The Diary of Another Nobody

Life in 1952

The Diary of Another Nobody
Life in 1952

from The Diaries of
Hubert Arthur Berry

RARE BOOKS AND BERRY
2007

This paperback edition published in 2007 by
Rare Books and Berry
High Street, Porlock,
Minehead, Somerset
TA24 8PT

First published in 2005 in Great Britain by Rare Books an Berry

www.rarebooksandberry.co.uk

A CIP catalogue record for this title is
Available from the British Library

ISBN 978-0-9539951-6-5

Designed and typeset in Minion at
Libanus Press, Marlborough

Printed and bound by
Biddles Ltd, King's Lynn

CONDITIONS OF SALE

All rights reserved. No part of this publication may be reproduced,
stored in a retrieval system, or transmitted in any form or by any means,
electronic, mechanical, photocopying, recording or otherwise, without
the prior permission of the publisher

This book is sold subject to the condition that it shall not, by way of trade
or otherwise, be lent, re-sold, hired out or otherwise circulated without the
publisher's prior consent in any form of binding or cover other than that in
which it is published and without a similar condition including this
condition being imposed on the subsequent purchaser

For Josh, Elsie, Alex, Chris, Katie and Milly

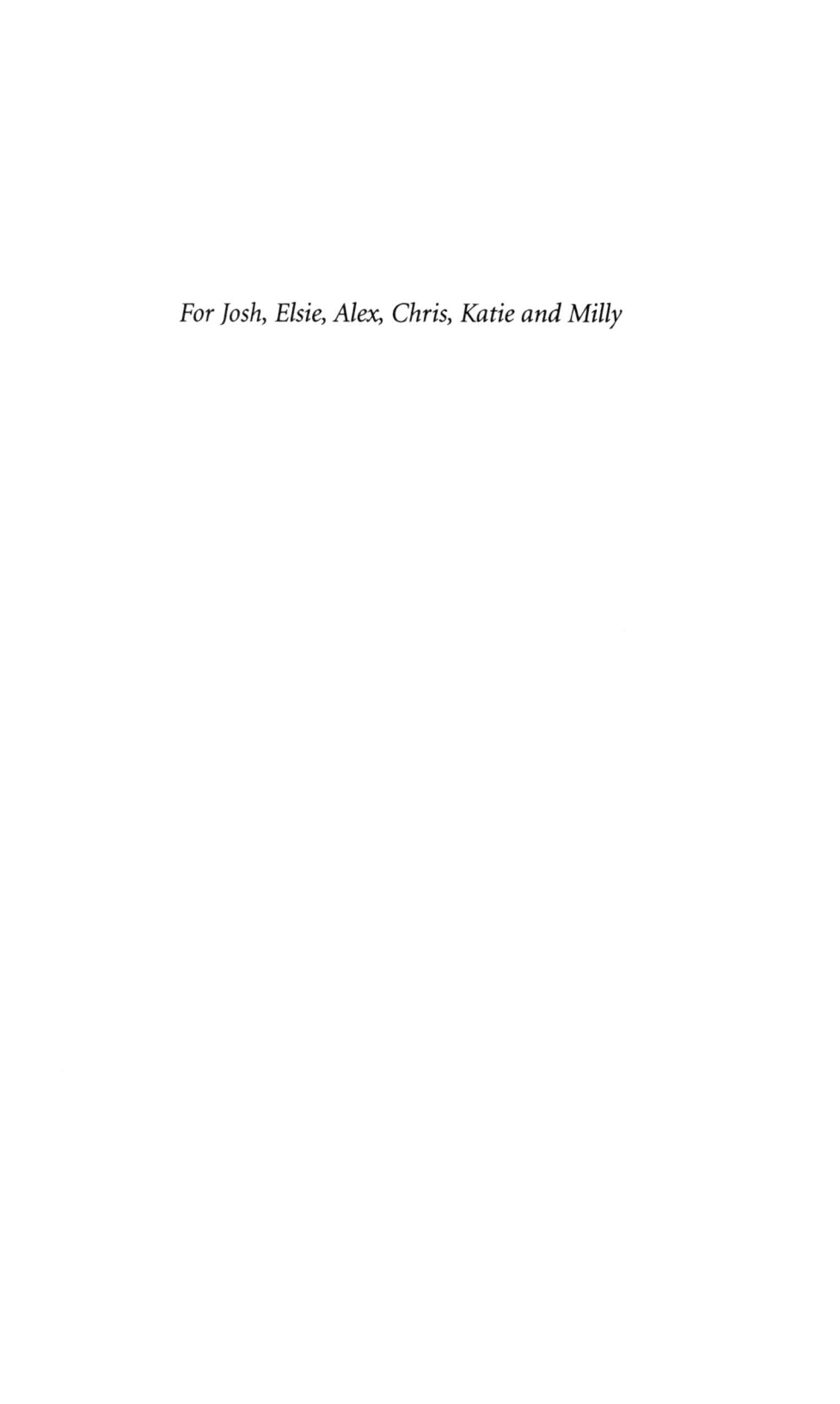

Foreword

This is how it was in 1952. No television, no car, no telephone. When reading this diary you might think bringing up a family in 1952, on the surface, seems idyllic, however financial worries were obviously there, a monthly deficit of £10-00 was recorded causing concern. Breeding budgerigars, cultivating the garden, keeping hens and growing tobacco was the only way to supplement the average monthly wage. Child birth at home with the help of the next door neighbour; baths once a week, a luxury. This was the norm, how times change in 50 years or so.

It all takes place in the small Buckinghamshire village of Flackwell Heath, which had then a bus service every twenty minutes and a nearby train station; a transport system that could take you shopping to the main town, High Wycombe and to the place of work four miles away.

The following pages are unabridged from a diary I found on my father's bookshelf, whether he will thank me for publishing it remains to be seen but certainly it must be a small part of social history.

The Diary

Main Persons

Audrey *Wife*

Mike *Son*

Dave *Son*

Gillian & Don *My sister and husband*

Peggy & John *Audrey's sister and husband*

Bill & Elsie *Audrey's parents*

George & Dorothy *Mother and Father*

Dick & Mac *School friend & wife*

Smith Family *Neighbours*

Mr & Mrs Smith

Frances

Gillian

Andy

Neil

Ethel & Lou *Audrey's aunts*

Gertie & Olive *My aunts*

Other persons *Villagers, work colleagues and friends*

Monday, 7th April 1952
Pouring this morning. What a miserable April so far. Sunday reset a lot of seeds that failed to germinate. Am taking Mike to his Nan Nan's this morning. Wondered should we buy an Easter present for Suzanne. The blossom is nearly out. Blast the rain!!

Tuesday, 8th April 1952
More rain today but mild. Outer case of cherry buds open. 9 or 10 young Budgies hatched out. If rain doesn't stop soon the lawn will be out of hand. Michael can almost (!) load and fire his popgun unaided. Everybody feeling very tired!! Except Michael!!!

Wednesday, 9th April 1952
Children next door played with Michael all the morning. He raked out the kitchen fire with the washing up mop. Very close and warm today, temperature in London reached 70°, followed by a thunderstorm here tonight. Cut grass for the first time this evening. Looking forward to the holiday and my birthday party on Friday.

Thursday, 10th April 1952
Birthday tomorrow. Worked all evening preparing. Audrey burnt tarts and spoilt cake – curse the cooker.

Friday, 11th April 1952 (Good Friday)
Two cars and a motor cycle combination in the drive for birthday party. Very successful. Nice pair of hedging shears from Bill. Easter Eggs for Mike. Lovely day – cut grass in the morning.

Saturday, 12th April 1952
Fine day but dull. Sowed H. A. Agrostemma. Clary (Salvia Bluebeard) and Cornflowers. Made draining board for Audrey.

Sunday, 13th April 1952 (Easter Day)
Glorious day. Basked in the sun, too hot to work in the afternoon. Cherry and damson blossom out. Planted main crop potatoes. Mike pulled up clematis. Mac and Dick for tea followed by my Mother and Audrey's Ma and Pa. Went for a pint with Bill.

Monday, 14th April 1952 (Easter Monday)
The finest and hottest Easter of the century. Mike went to my Mother's for the day. Plum and cherry blossom out. Nearly all seeds planted. Visited by Gill and Don with née March and husband 2.30pm and they hadn't had lunch!! 14 Budgies hatched.

Tuesday, 15th April 1952
Another fine day. Mike went to his Nan Nan's while Audrey did the washing. Blossom in the cherry full out. 15 Budgies hatched. Great Tits building in stink pipe. Work was awful!

Wednesday, 16th April 1952
Another fine day. Discovered slugs were eating seedlings so put down slug killer. Cut grass for second time. Hard work and have decided to save up for motor mower.

Thursday, 17th April 1952
Another Budgie hatched but 2 die! Pear blossom coming out. Mike made us roar with his pipe and cough act. Cutting the grass until dark. Caught a lot of slugs!

Friday, 18th April 1952
Another marvellous today. Heard cuckoo this morning.

Saturday, 19th April 1952
Yet another wonderful day. Mike and I were about without shirts or vests most of the day. Started work on the lawn under the cherry tree. The Flowering Cherry is just blossoming. Planted our various shrubs and set Marigold seeds.

Sunday, 20th April 1952
Another fine day. Saw the view over the Thames for the first time. Another bird hatched out. Started to prepare the ground for grass under the cherry tree. The cherry blossom is past its best. Another Budgie – 15 in all. Michael went to see Andy's newts. Mike moved chair when Audrey about to sit down – crash!

Monday, 21st April 1952
   Went to Shillingford Bridge Hotel, Victor's farewell party. Got home 12.30am, not tight. Hit Cecil the cesspool souser en voyage. Poured all day. Audrey did spring cleaning. Another Budgie, 16 in all.

Tuesday, 22nd April 1952
   Discovered 2 blue Budgies. Showery weather. Cherry blossom nearly over. Strong wind last night blew off lot of apple fruit spurs.

Wednesday, 23rd April 1952
   Showery weather. Budgie died, leaves 15. Not being fed. Audrey bought a coat from Maidenhead – went with Mother and Peggy and Mike. Tom Tit (Great Tit) in the kitchen this morning.

Thursday, 24th April 1952
   Cut some of the grass tonight. Audrey saw doctor. Query August or September. Baby to be born at home. Bought 12½ lbs bird seed. Took watch to be cleaned. 6 weeks to wait so shan't have it for holiday.

Friday, 25th April 1952
   Completed grass cutting. Audrey trimmed edges. Fine sunny day. Slight frost this morning. Lots of apple blossom in pink bud stage. Bill sprayed his apples with lime sulphur.

Saturday, 26th April 1952
   Audrey's Mother's birthday party. Very good tea – chicken, trifle and ice cream. Bought Mike a pusher – he thinks it's a new toy. His catchword at the moment is BIG SPIDER!

Sunday, 27th April 1952
   Beautiful day. Working in the garden without a shirt. Finished the lawn making. Audrey helped. My father fetched Mike for the afternoon and brought us a cake. The ornamental cherry is nearly out. Budgies thriving. Penstemon seeds have germinated, also Dianthus.

Monday, 28th April 1952
Audrey succeeded in burning out the oven elements, what a foul smell! She also laid some lino in the lavatory and Mike's bedroom.

Tuesday, 29th April 1952
Audrey and Mike and I went to Gill and Don's. Beautiful day, hot and sunny. Gill and Don have been doing their garden and Don has got some vegetables in.

Wednesday, 30th April 1952
Fine day with thunderstorm at night. 10lbs Budgie mixture arrives. Rose at 6.20am and did some weeding. Mike has spent all day in the garden and has been very good.

Thursday, 1st May 1952
Woke up feeling as though I had flu. Feel better tonight. Visited Mars with LCS and had coffee at his house on the way back. Showery weather. No gardening tonight as I haven't felt like it and weeds growing like mad. Howland will take all the Budgies.

Friday, 2nd May 1952
Showery violent rain at times. Dick asked us to mind their dog, Incline, for the weekend while they go to Burton.

Saturday, 3rd May 1952
Showery weather. Did painting and odd job – no gardening. Took Mike to enquire about trains to Bournemouth. Incline is quite a handful to control. Went with Audrey and Mike to Crooked Billet for ½ pint. Heard Mr Churchill's party political broadcast – more economy and more houses.

Sunday, 4th May 1952
Poured with rain most of the day. Cloud burst at midday. Painted the kitchen cupboard door. Mike, Punch and Incline nearly drove me mad! Incline had me up at 3.30am this morning. He escaped from great chains and out of the shed! Aunt Ethel's meat was very nice today. Scrounged together hankies and a card for Rosemary's 21st birthday and made an envelope. Olive hen out today!

Monday, 5th May 1952
> Showery and rather chilly. Cut grass at front – hard work. Pricked out tobacco plants into cold frame (Amarillo). Another egg in one of the Budgie nests. No more young out, I think it must be too cold. Mike went to Nan Nan's. Audrey spring cleaned Mike's and the spare bedroom. They look better!

Tuesday, 6th May 1952
> Showery and rather cold again. Rather worried about Apple Blossom which is beginning to fall and no bees about at all. Peg and John came this evening. We had a nice tea and discussed ways of making money – reached no conclusions. Another Budgie out. Gave John some Amarillo seedlings.

Wednesday, 7th May 1952
> Fine day but chilly. Lawn grass is coming up. 3 more Budgies out, 7 in all. Another egg. Bill didn't fetch Audrey's mother because they are expecting Aunt Ethel. Audrey did a lot of weeding. Planted more tobacco seedlings.

Thursday, 8th May 1952
> Showery and rather chilly. Bramley blossom practically fallen. Caught 6 young Budgies and put them in separate cage in aviary. My Mother came up and took Mike to see Goosey Gander. Ordered immersion heater.

Friday, 9th May 1952
> Fine day at last. Audrey had a perm and bought a new skirt. Another Budgie out – ordered 10lbs seed. Enquired about Punch at Misvine Kennels for boarding out during holiday. The place stunk!

Saturday, 10th May 1952
> Fine warm day. Weeding this morning. Went to Loudwater to tea. Aunt Olive staying with my Mother for the weekend. Went to Beaconsfield Fair. Mike went on the roundabouts with me and by himself. Audrey won a pair of earrings. Walked home. Arranged for Punch to go to Highland Kennels.

Sunday, 11th May 1952

Fine spells and violent showers all day. Did nothing in the garden but weeding except to split the Polyanthus. Went for a short walk this afternoon. The Broom is in flower. Audrey's Mother and Father bought Mike a red blazer yesterday. Punch seems better behaved just lately.

Monday, 12th May 1952

Showery weather again – ground very wet. Set runner beans. 2 eggs in old hen's nest, 3 eggs in yellow cock's nest. Mike went to his Nan Nan's today. Audrey spring cleaned the hall. Wrote asking for cesspool to be emptied.

Tuesday, 13th May 1952

Fine warm day. Audrey's Mother and Father brought us Aster, Heliotrope, Stocks and Petunia plants. Cleared out Wallflowers and set them. Set more lettuce and beetroot. Broad beans are setting well.

Wednesday, 14th May 1952

Fine warm day. More weeding and lashing down of grass. Went for a pint with Bill. He lent me his watch. An egg in the young olive hen's nest. The hawthorn hedges need cutting. Things are growing at a terrific rate this year. Sent Gill some pants for her birthday.

Thursday, 15th May 1952

Fine warm day. Cut grass. Gill and Don and my Mother came up this evening. Audrey went with them for a ride round – Winter Hill, Hurley and a drink at the King's Head, Little Marlow.

Friday, 16th May 1952

Beautiful warm day. Audrey bought sandals and a shirt for Mike. Howland is collecting 15 young birds Tuesday at 2.30pm at £1 each. Cut grass and scythed a lot of the long stuff. The Flowering Cherry is virtually over.

Saturday, 17th May 1952
Hottest May day for 81 years (according to the Sunday Express). Mike and I went about without shirts. I have got a slightly burned back. Booked the tickets this morning, £2.17.4d. Weeding and hoeing, sprayed greenfly with Clensill. First of the Peonies out. Tea on the lawn.

Sunday, 18th May 1952
Another marvellous hot day. Best weekend of the year so far. Set a row of Giant Stude peas. Hoed and weeded. Staked delphiniums. Mike was collected by my Father at 11.30am for the day. Nearly finished the packing. Tea on the lawn.

Monday, 19th May 1952
Very hot and oppressive day – terrible at work. Thunderstorm with heavy rain this evening. Put all the young birds – 15 in the crate for Howland. Mike went to his Nan Nan's. Audrey sprung clean the lavatory and bathroom. Insurance man called. I bought pair of sandals 29/9d.

Tuesday, 20th May 1952
Wet day. £15 for birds!! Railway collected trunk. Prepared ground for brussels. Audrey set sweet corn in shrubbery. Heard nightingale this evening. Apples are setting well and plums look exceptional. 7 eggs in yellow cock's nest. Mike looking forward to seaside.

Wednesday, 21st May 1952
Fine cool day. Cut grass this evening and planted out a few Brussels, Cambridge No 1 and 5 mixed. Propped up a limb of the plum tree because it is so laden. Tobacco plants are growing well.

Thursday, 22nd May 1952
Fine warm day. Weather forecast good. Visitors tonight. Audrey's Mum and Pop, my Mother, Gill and Don. Cut grass. All ready for holiday. Mac sent two sundresses for Audrey to borrow and Gill also brought a dress.

Friday, 23rd May 1952
Fine warm day. Weather forecast excellent! Everything ready and organised to leave tomorrow. Looking forward to it. Garden in good order. Broad beans will be ready to pick when we come back. A prolonged series of explosions at 9.45pm near Loudwater. Some is machine gun fire for certain. No siren. Took Punch to Highland Kennels – seems OK.

Saturday, 24th May 1952
The explosions were fireworks!!

Thursday, 5th June 1952
Cesspool emptied.

Friday, 6th June 1952
Finished cutting the front hedge.

Saturday, 7th June 1952
Lovely day. Went to Marlow and ordered cooker. Received bird seed from Howland. Planted out Antirrinhum and Ageratum. Still catching up in the garden from the holiday. Went to garden fete at May Place. Cut the grass – first time since before the holiday. Planted tomatoes 'The Amateur'.

Sunday, 8th June 1952
Fine this morning but poured all day without ceasing from noon. Nearly straight at the front. Peg and John came for tea. Peggy brought lovely strawberry flan she had made. Gave John some tobacco plants. Mike did his head over heels to entertain the guests.

Monday, 9th June 1952
Dull but dry day. Mike went to his Nan Nan's for the day. Audrey finished painting the cupboard. Planted out a row of white sprouting. The Witch Hazel has been snapped off – mended it with adhesive tape and grafting wax, hoping for the best. Broke garden fork – damn – another £1.

Tuesday, 10th June 1952
Fine warm day. Set Sweet William and Cherianthum seeds broadcast. Gill and Don came for supper. Listened to big fight. Turpin beat Cockell.

Wednesday, 11th June 1952
Fine warm day. Broke border fork tonight. The blue and yellow Budgies seem queer. 10 cwts anthracite delivered. Audrey's Mother and Father came up this evening.

Thursday, 12th June 1952
Fine warm day. Mike wears his bathing costume these days. Planted 12 Coleus. Audrey disapproved of them. John came for some plants – broccoli etc. He is painting his motorbike.

Friday, 13th June 1952
Dull damp day. Income tax rebate £8.17. All spent on goodness knows what. Digging and weeding in the garden.

Saturday 14th June 1952
Dull rather miserable day. Weeding and digging. Planted out curly kale, broccoli Walcheren and January King. Tomato plants. Sowed lettuce and carrots. Transplanted swedes. Went to my Mother's for tea. Mike very good. He has developed the habit of climbing out of his cot and coming into our bedroom in the mornings.

Sunday, 15th June 1952
Dull day but fine evening. Weeding and digging this morning. Mac, Dick and Suzanne for tea. Mike likes Suzanne. Went for a drink with Dick this evening. The Mayhews rolled up about 10 and stayed until midnight!!

Monday, 16th June 1952
Fine day. Cherries are ripening. It is quite a good crop. Much better than last year.

Tuesday, 17th June 1952
   Dull and dry, rather chilly. Stan and Bridget's for tea – Mike behaved very well. Bridget is going to have a baby in January. The nurse left a note to say she had found a woman to look after Audrey. Cut grass under cherry tree.

Wednesday, 18th June 1952
   Cold, windy, miserable day. Set Geums, Antirrinhums, Stocks. Crane called for an order – has sold no Budgies. Mike woke at 3 this morning and tried to come in our bed. Feel tired out tonight.

Thursday, 19th June 1952
   Stayed away from work with a cold on my chest. Audrey went into the town and fixed up with the Electricity people about the cooker.

Friday, 20th June 1952
   Went to work, feel awful. Went to Dr Low in the evening. Went for a pint with Bill afterwards! Raspberries are coming on. They have done well for first year.

Saturday, 21st June 1952
   Dull day. Didn't do much all day. Picked cherries for my Father in the evening.

Sunday, 22nd June 1952
   Dull day. Still didn't feel too grand. No gardening. Went to Peg's birthday party. Strawberry flan, homemade meat pie, fruit trifle, cream cakes, sponge etc etc for tea. Forgot my medicine and John brought it along afterwards! Cornus, silver and gold, are nice variegated leaf shrubs in Peg's garden. Audrey's Mother recommends Lychnis HP.

Monday, 23rd June 1952
   Feel a bit better today. Weather fine and warm. Haven't smoked since Wednesday. Cherries about half way over. Planted out purple sprouting. Mike went to his Nan Nan's as usual.

Tuesday, 24th June 1952
Fine warm day. Still feel a bit queer. Started to cut grass. Audrey did edges. Hundreds of small apples have fallen – the weather has been quite windy. Picking raspberries. They are very good. Howland delivered and said he had sold all the birds.

Wednesday, 25th June 1952
Fine hot day. Feel a lot better today. Picked cherries this evening. John came up to help. We picked about 20lbs and John took 10lbs. Punch ate the ones that fell on the ground.

Thursday, 26th June 1952
Fine hot day. Terribly close. Continued cutting grass. Myrtle visited us this evening. Audrey's Mother looked after Mike while Audrey visited doctor. He still can't say whether it's August or September. Cooker installed.

Friday, 27th June 1952
Fine hot day. Audrey's Mother and Father go to Branscombe tomorrow. Finished cutting grass. The hardy annuals are not making much progress, too dry. Had tea in the garden. Howland has agreed to take Budgies 22nd July for 17/6d each.

Saturday, 28th June 1952
Roasting hot day. Must be lovely at Branscombe. Mike and I in bathing costumes. Desultory work in garden. Went to Wycombe in the morning and took mangle to be mended. Went to garden fete at Sedgmoor House. Wonderful gardens and view. Mike met Andy there and they had a good time.

Sunday, 29th June 1952
Another boiling day. Audrey can't stand the heat. Mike and I in bathing costumes all day. All stuffing lovely ripe cherries and Mike playing with baths and buckets of water. Mr Smith topped his nut tree – gave me quite a lump. Make good firewood. Sky blue Budgie attacked by old green hen so we had sent latter to solitary confinement. The Spiraea Waterii is flowering.

Monday, 30th June 1952
Boiling scorching day. No gardening tonight. Started relining pram. Mike has a slight cold and touch of diarrhoea – may be from eating cherries yesterday.

Tuesday, 1st July 1952
Boiling scorching day again. Audrey is flaked out. Mike and Punch carry on as usual. Finished relining pram and dismantled it for cleaning and touching up. Cleaned out back room and burnt miles of junk. Watered the garden extensively – expect it will rain.

Wednesday, 2nd July 1952
Cooler today, thank goodness. Eddie and Margaret to tea. No gardening. Went to Audrey's Mother's at dinner time. Hectic day at work. Mike slept on divan of his own accord dinner time.

Thursday, 3rd July 1952
Wet, cold and miserable day. Amazing weather. We could do with a fire. No gardening tonight. Started cleaning pram. Evelyn couldn't come. She sent a telegram which Jennings brought through the wood to say her husband had been taken ill.

Friday, 4th July 1952
Cold this morning but warm again in the afternoon. My cold has come back a bit, confound it. The nest of blue Budgies was attacked – we think by mice and all the young ones killed. The old hen we isolated has escaped – 17/6d down the drain – plus the young ones – blast!!

Saturday, 5th July 1952
The weather is boiling hot again. The rain on Thursday has had little or no effect. Took pram hood and apron for recovering to Currys. Planted out Savoys and watered – peas, tomatoes and marrow. Swept up a barrow load of June drop apples.

Sunday, 6th June 1952
Very hot and close. Desultory work in garden. The Spiraea is full out. It will be interesting to see how long it lasts. Sowed Pansies and Violas. Wrote to Audrey's Mother and Father at Branscombe. Had first picking of green peas.

Monday, 7th June 1952
Cooler today and quite windy this evening. Have bottled 9lb bottles of Tantarium cherries. Sowed a row of Arctic King in the hopes of a winter supply. This proved successful. Fine lettuce for Mike's birthday party. Audrey made 7 delicious cherry turnovers this evening.

Tuesday, 8th July 1952
Cooler but fine – nice evening. We badly need rain. Nurse came today and left packet of sterilized instruments. Worked in garden cutting down dead flowers, staking and watering. Started to clear centre bed ready for turfing.

Wednesday, 9th July 1952
Fine day. Started to dig out patch in centre of garden. Mrs Foster, 17 Buckingham Way, called yesterday and offered to come from 8am until 3-3.30pm for 2 guineas per week.

Thursday, 10th July 1952
Fine day, very dry. Gill and Don and my Mother visited us this evening. Gillian borrowed Mike's picture.

Friday, 11th July 1952
Dull day with heavy rain this evening at last. I have done practically nothing in the garden for the last few days. The Giant Stride peas are bearing very well. Gave Pat 2 weeks notice today.

Saturday, 12th July 1952
Dull day, rather chilly. Did odd jobs around and about. Finished pram, painted copper etc. Cleared a bit more of the centre bed at the front. Picked a few cherries which are black now. Raspberries are over. One lot of damsons are changing colour.

Sunday, 13th July 1952
Bright day but very strong wind blowing. Audrey's Mother and Father came up in the afternoon. They are brown and had a very good holiday. We had various presents of Devon pottery and material for the baby's nightdresses. Mike has been very good today but was rather excited tonight. Took cuttings of Golden Privet, Cotoneaster, Fuschia and Pinks.

Monday, 14th July 1952
Dull and fine. Budgie taken ill. Don't think it will survive. Caught birds ready for Howland tomorrow. 15 in all. Bird seed delivered. Audrey started spring cleaning kitchen.

Tuesday, 15th July 1952
Dull and fine. We still need rain very badly. Mike went to see chicks next door. Howland hasn't been although Audrey has spent the money – in theory at any rate. Still clearing out the centre patch.

Wednesday, 16th July 1952
Fine day with wind getting up this evening. Budgie died. Very busy at work with Eddie on holiday. Cut down old canes among raspberries. Watered them and plum tree with cesspool water. Audrey making nightdresses for the baby.

Thursday, 17th July 1952
Dull day with showers although not enough to do any good. Susan and Judith and Evelyn visited Audrey for the day – all went well. Mike enjoyed having the playmates. Budded a briar with Dorothy Perkins – not too hopeful.

Friday, 18th July 1952
Fine.

Saturday, 19th July 1952
Fine hot day. Spent nearly all day at Mac and Dick's doing nothing. Suzanne is very well. Mike was very good.

Sunday, 20th July 1952
    Fine hot day. Did a few odd jobs but it is very warm for gardening. We very badly need rain. The Early Rivers plums are on the verge of ripeness. Saw a wasp for the first time today. Audrey and I went for a walk to Bourne End this evening while my Mother and Father babysat. We caught the bus back and had a pint at the Happy Union!

Monday, 21st July 1952
    Fine day – very close and muggy and unpleasant at work. Spent evening watering – particularly the Victoria plum with water from the cesspool. Took Mike to his Nan Nan's and had lift home in Mr George's Sunbeam Talbot. Howland fetches birds tomorrow.

Tuesday, 22nd July 1952
    Fine hot day. Stan and Bridget to tea. Mike was a bit hot and choppered. Not on his best behaviour. Howland didn't turn up for the birds which is rather disappointing. Very hot in bed these nights.

Wednesday, 23rd July 1952
    Fine warm day. Mr Francis came this evening to put the immersion heater in. Unfortunately it leaks a bit but I hope to be able to stop it. Watered things in the garden from the cesspool – what a stink. Bill says John's tobacco plants are bigger than mine.

Thursday, 24th July 1952
    Fine warm day. The immersion heater seems to have stopped leaking. Swept up windfall apples and watered tobacco plants. My Mother came up and said Gill and Don had been given 3 weeks notice because the school is closing.

Friday, 25th July 1952
    Fine hot day – very close. Garden is dying for rain. Pat went today. Gill and Don came up this evening. Offered to let them have a caravan in the garden and store furniture here for 3 or 4 months.

Saturday, 26th July 1952
Fine hot day with a cooler wind tonight. Walked to Loudwater over Golflinks this afternoon. Spent the evening watering. The so-called Early Rivers plum is quite ripe and the large blue plum not far away.

Sunday, 27th July 1952
Dry but dull and rather chilly. Mike is generally good but he does like his own way. He shouts through the fence for Andy until they have to get him. Dug all the Home Guard potatoes after some of the larger ones appeared rather brown inside. There must have been almost 1½ cwts.

Monday, 28th July 1952
Dull and chilly but rain holding off. Went to see Mr Baker. He gave me a pot plant 'Inpatiens Balsam' and recommended Laxtons Exquisite. Mike has a cold – hope it won't be much – he seems alright in himself.

Tuesday, 29th July 1952
Fine day – warmer. Still no rain. Mike's cold is no worse. Stayed late at work with Eddie who came home for supper. Watered tobacco plants which are growing quite well.

Wednesday, 30th July 1952
Fine close weather. Terrific panic tonight – we think it's coming! Dashing down to the bottom shed at dead of night to fetch the chamber!!

Thursday, 31st July 1952
Fine and dry. Nothing happened last night after all – thank goodness. Started to prepare the back porch for snow cem. Had a picking of beans for dinner tonight. The dry weather hasn't helped the beans so far.

Saturday, 2nd August 1952
Showers today. Finished the back porch.

Sunday, 3rd August 1952
Shower again today. Desultory jobs in the garden. Bottled the small and large plums. Went for a walk to the Crooked Billet and over the hills to Heath End. Had a drink at The Stag while my Mother minded Michael. Had our first picking of beans today.

Monday, 4th August 1952 (Bank Holiday)
Another showery day. April weather. Audrey did her washing and I finished clearing the large bed at the front. Went to Turville with Audrey's Mum and Dad and came back home for tea. The garden is much better for the rain. Mike's cold has nearly gone.

Tuesday, 5th August 1952
Showers again. The garden is responding well. Planted out Heleniums and Bocconia. The new girl started today. Her typing is disappointing.

Wednesday, 6th August 1952
Showers again with a VIOLENT thunderstorm tonight which put the lights out – Audrey's Mum and Pop here. Pop suggested Audrey might have her baby so I dashed along to phone. Telephone not working, they say they will mend the line tonight. Put a washer in the top cistern which was leaking. The grass is coming quite green again already. We've had beans every day since Sunday.

Thursday, 7th August 1952
Another showery day with rain all this evening. My Mother came for plums but too wet to pick. Did an odd bit of painting in the kitchen. Shall have to get the lawn mower out when it dries. Wrote for cesspool to be emptied.

Friday, 8th August 1952
Showers and wet this evening. Had to stake the Brussels which are very large. Lots of apples falling off with the wind and rain. Sold 2 yellow Budgies (pair) for 35/-.

Saturday, 9th August 1952

Showers and terrific downpours all day. Water gushing over spouts and porches like waterfalls. The same man arrived at 8.15am! for 2 more Budgies (35/-). Electrician fixed immersion heater which seems very good. Went to Maidenhead to flog more birds, without success. Must ring Abbots Tuesday, Maidenhead 217 (pet shop).

Sunday, 10th August 1952

Drier today with sunny spells. Blowing half a gale however and there are literally hundreds of apples off this weekend. They are too sour for cooking. We have had a few Worcester Pearmans for eating which aren't bad. Odd jobs about the house and weeding in the garden. Mike has been very good. He still smokes his pipe and gabbles like mad but is very hard to understand. Mac and Dick came up for a few minutes. They bought Mike a nice shirt for a boy of 6. He can wear it too!

Monday, 11th August 1952

Dull and dry although the wireless forecast rain. Cut the grass at the front tonight. The first time since 27th June. Mike went to his Nan Nan's. Had another bath. The heater is very good – it takes 1hr 45 mins to get the whole tank really hot.

Tuesday, 12th August 1952

Better weather today. Sold 11 Budgies to Abbots at Maidenhead. Audrey will take them over tomorrow. Very busy day at work arranging to send part of a job to Holland (Baron Encore).

Wednesday, 13th August 1952

Fine day. Audrey took Budgies to Maidenhead. She had to wait hours for the buses. Cheque for £4.2.6d. Cut the grass under the cherry tree. Gave Audrey's Mother plants and plums. Mike went next door – we'ed in their garden – made Frances cry and let the chickens out – so he said.

Thursday, 14th August 1952

Audrey woke me at 3.30am with pains. They have been going on all day. Mac and Dick came and the nurse called at 9.30pm. Audrey had a hot bath and castor oil.

Friday, 15th August 1952
Stormy day. The pains have continued unceasingly all night and all day. The nurse has been twice. Unfortunately there is another patient in the same condition who has the gas and air. Mike has gone to his Nan Nan's tonight. At the moment Audrey is in a hot bath and there is a thunderstorm without rain in progress. The lights keep dipping and I have mustered all available candles.

Saturday, 16th August 1952
At 3.30am this morning Audrey thought it was coming. I was all ready to fetch the nurse but it gradually passed off. During the rest of the day nothing happened at all. We went for a drink in the evening! There was a terrible storm in North Devon last night and the village of Lynmouth was half washed away by floods when the River Lyn changed course.

Sunday, 17th August 1952
This morning is fine but chilly. Audrey feels as thought the baby is a month away and we are going to get Mike back this afternoon. It has been, I think, the most beautiful day of the summer. The garden has really looked nice. Mike came back this afternoon and has gone to bed in the divan for the first time. My Father came up this evening. As we are gong to bed tonight Audrey has the pains again. Ordered 12 bush roses from Cuthberts. There was 9 ins of rain in Lynmouth on Friday.

Monday, 18th August 1952
Thoroughly wet all day. No signs of anything.

Tuesday, 19th August 1952
Better day today. Audrey has had no more pains. Don came up this evening to say Gill is ill in bed and my Mother is off to Booker. My Father is away at Avonmouth. Planted out Tree Lupins and Cherianthus.

Wednesday, 20th August 1952
Dry and dull. No news from my Mother or Gill. Audrey still the same but feeling very fit. Cut the grass at the front. Fuschia in full flower. Convolvulus reach to the top of the porch but haven't flowered yet. Mike has been playing 'mothers and fathers' with Frances.

Thursday, 21st August 1952

Fine sunny day. Cut the oval grass at the front. Punch has the roving spirit again so he has been tied up today.

Friday, 22nd August 1952

Fine and warm today. Gill and Don and Mac and Dick came up this evening. Gillian is better but not well yet. Went for a pint with Dick. Audrey went into the town today. She is keeping very well. No gardening tonight. Cesspool emptied today.

Saturday, 23rd August 1952

Lovely day. Audrey still well. Mike has been quite good. Did odd jobs and hoed some of the weeds. Gill and Don came for tea. Don took Audrey and me to Chalfont St Giles to the 'Merlins Cave' – such cobwebs, and to St Peter to the 'Greyhound'. Gill doesn't look too good yet. The Red Hot Pokers are nearly over. The Fuschia continues in full flower.

Sunday, 24th August 1952

Another nice day. This has been a shorts and singlet weekend. Mike has had terrific energy and go today. Nearly driven us potty. Started filling in the centre bed with earth preparation to grassing. Seed or sods? Picked our third marrow in 3 weeks. All have been very big. Audrey feels a bit 'heavy' tonight and we are hoping it may lead to something. She went out with her Mum and Pop to Marlow Common and brought back a few roots of heather – which we have planted.

Monday, 25th August 1952

Another fine, warm day. Audrey still well and kicking. Isn't Monday awful. Planted out more Cherianthus.

Tuesday, 26th August 1952

Hot humid day. Nothing much to report. It is dark now at 8.30pm, worse luck. Bottled Victorias and damsons.

Wednesday, 27th August 1952
   Hot and warm, turning dull and very windy this evening. Started drying the bottom leaves of my tobacco plants in the bottom shed. Don came up to say that Gill had gone to Oxford for a few days and invited me to the HWCC Sausage Supper.

Thursday, 28th August 1952
   Hot and warm again today. The Convolvulus major bloomed today – very pretty but the flowers only last a few hours. Tomatoes ripening.

Friday, 29th August 1952
   Hot and warm. Started cutting the front grass again. Went with Don to the Cricket Club Sausage Supper to celebrate the choice of Alf Hughes and David Johns for the Minor Counties game against the Indians. Ben Barnet was there – ex-Australian test wicket keeper.

Saturday, 30th August 1952
   Warm, close and thundery. Cut grass and fiddled in the front garden all day. My Father came up this evening – so Mike has to fall over the garden gate onto his face – rather badly bruised and grazed, poor kid. He seems alright this evening and is sleeping well. He soon gets over these things. Next door left on holiday.

Sunday, 31st August 1952
   Dull warm day. Spent the morning cutting the Smith side hedge and preparing the old rose bed for grass. Mike has got over his fall alright but looks a bit of a mess. Audrey's father came up this morning and brought the pusher back. My Mother and Father came up after tea. My Father took some plums and damsons for Ealing. Peg and John came later and stayed the evening. Quite a visited day. It's a pity the summer is passing – it is dark at 8.15pm now!

Monday, 1st September 1952
   Fine day. Planted out Canterbury Bells.

Tuesday, 2nd September 1952
Fine day again. Went to Peg and John's for tea. Discussed tobacco plants and John's patent weed extractor! Mike's face is getting better.

Wednesday, 3rd September 1952
Dull day. We could do with a drop of rain. Finished off old rose bed ready for turfs. Mike is still very scabby. Audrey keeping very fit.

Thursday, 4th September 1952
Dull day, rather cold. Audrey went to see the doctor who told her any minute now and gave some horrible pills. We are building up to another panic. My mother came up this evening. Gill is better now but apparently doesn't look too good. Mike's face is almost better.

Friday, 5th September 1952
Sunny and dry but very cold for the time of the year. Planted out Aquilegia and Sweet Williams. Lifted the onions – about 10 or 12lbs – small bulbs. Sold Gillian two Budgies – blue and yellow, for 15/-. They are going to Jordans and will have to store furniture here.

Saturday, 6th September 1952
Dry and rather cold and dull. Audrey has felt a bit off colour today. Mike has been very good. Lifted King Edwards – about ½ cwt from 14lbs. Picked all the Victorias and all the damsons. Picked blackberries and made 6lb blackberry and apple jam. Next door came back from their holiday today. The Fuschia is still blooming strongly. Sent fee for tobacco curing and hung some more leaves.

Sunday, 7th September 1952
Rained all day. Audrey's father brought us about 3lbs blackberries today! This afternoon we went to Loudwater. Very little progress at all. The weather is cold and we could do with a fire. Must get crates for apples and arrange for sale of Budgies.

Monday, 8th September 1952
    Fine today. Mike went to his Nan Nan's. Mac and Dick came this evening – we lent them the playpen and high chair for Suzanne. She can stand on her own now – but hasn't any teeth yet. Mac doesn't look her old self yet.

Tuesday, 9th September 1952
    Damp, dull and still cold. Very poor weather for the time of the year. Nurse Cobb called (HW 1886). Grease banded trees and sowed Arctic King lettuce.

Wednesday, 10th September 1952
    Better day today – not so cold. Audrey's Mother came up as usual. She and Bill stayed talking until 9. She has made us a very nice rug for the front room. We have a good lot of Brussels – there is a picking available already.

Thursday, 11th September 1952
    Fine day but unable to do anything this evening because of rain. Getting a bit worried about harvesting tobacco, apples and tomatoes.

Friday, 12th September 1952
    Fine day. Planted out Wallflowers.

Saturday, 13th September 1952
    Fine warm day at last. Sat in the sun this afternoon. Picked and hung another batch of tobacco leaves. Cut grass at back and planted out Bellis Wallflowers and Sweet Williams. Doctor called and said he will make baby come on Tuesday.

Sunday, 14th September 1952
    Fine day. Castor oil – hot bath. No effect.

Monday, 15th September 1952
    Fine day. Picked fourth batch of tobacco. The rest are drying well.

Tuesday, 16th September 1952
D Day. Fine and sunny. Lovely day. Baby born at between 5.00 and 5.30pm. No nurse or anaesthetic. Doctor arrived just in time to deliver it. Mrs Smith saved situation. I arrived home just as it was coming, to find no doctor or nurse and everyone in a panic – except Audrey. Nothing I could do. However, all is well.

Wednesday, 17th September 1952
Dull and rain this evening. Stayed home this morning. Audrey and David (Roger) doing well. My Mother, Gill and Don came up this evening. Have got a few drinks in to celebrate. Mrs Foster is very good. David is a bit niggly this evening. Hope he sleeps well!

Thursday, 18th September 1952
Fine day. All well. Very cold last night. Up at 5.45am because of it. Lots of visitors. Furniture stored. Planted out spring cabbage and uprooted and put under cover all tobacco plants. Thanked neighbours for assistance. Gave Nurse Cobb some apples. £5 from Audrey's Mother and Father. £1 from Peg and John. Gill moved today.

Friday, 19th September 1952
Fine day but rain this evening. David is very good and doesn't cry. Hung more tobacco leaves. Audrey's Mother and Mike came up this afternoon. Feel tired tonight. Expect a lot of visitors this weekend. Mike is enjoying himself at Nan Nan's and is looking forward to a car ride to Risborough tomorrow.

Saturday, 20th September 1952
Beautiful sunny day. Audrey and David doing well. Cut the grass at the front and hung more tobacco leaves. Peg and John came in the afternoon for a while and I went for a drink with Don in the evening.

Sunday, 21st September 1952

Another fine day. I cooked the dinner and it wasn't too bad. Made a Norfolk pudding. Picked the pears by the gate but fear they may have been left too long. Have hung nearly all the tobacco. Uprooted a whole root of the Amateur tomato. It must weigh 20lbs – and have hung it in the shed to see if it will ripen. Rather surprised that Audrey's Mother and Pop haven't been up with Mike.

Monday, 22nd September 1952

Fine sunny day. Audrey and David well. Audrey's Mother brought Mike to see Audrey this afternoon. Hung the balance of the tobacco.

Tuesday, 23rd September 1952

Fine sunny day again. Audrey's Mother, Mike and Mrs Agar here this afternoon. Clipped the edges of the grass. In several minds whether to start picking apples.

Wednesday, 24th September 1952

Dull day with almost a gale blowing this evening. Went to London today. Lunched with Marshall & Co and took 11 Budgies to Langs. Mr Smith next door took me in his car. Audrey is out of bed quite a bit now – almost too much I think!

Thursday, 25th September 1952

Dull wet day with another gale tonight. Started picking Newton Wonders – hundreds have fallen. Audrey and David doing well. Audrey's Mother and Peggy came up this afternoon. Punch has got a bad foot.

Friday, 26th September 1952

Fine day but cold. I believe it has been one of the coldest Septembers recorded. Picked more Newton Wonders – a long job and it is dark at 7.30pm now. David will get hiccups which is a nuisance.

Saturday, 27th September 1952
> Fine day, still very cold. Fetched Mike this morning for the weekend. He likes David. Hugs and kisses him. But what a row when they are both crying. Planted out Wallflowers, Pansies, Gypsophila and Antirrinhums. Picked a few more apples. David went out for the first time. Took him to the end of the road.

Sunday, 28th September 1952
> Terribly wet afternoon and evening. Mike spent the day at my Mothers. Chicken for dinner! Mrs Jefferies came up in the evening to nurse the baby. She has bought a very nice pram cover.

Monday, 29th September 1952
> Dry but very cold. Picked a few more apples from the tree outside the kitchen window. I think these are the first of the cookers to ripen.

Tuesday, 30th September 1952
> Beastly wet day. Went with YMPs to Thames Board Mills – lunch at Strand Palace. Arrived home at 8.30pm.

Wednesday, 1st October 1952
> Another shocking day. Nothing to report except that I brought back Mike tonight. He takes all the chopping and changing for granted.

Thursday, 2nd October 1952
> Another dull damp day. Order from Rivetts for 12 Budgies. Registered David's birth this evening. Announced that tea is to be de-rationed on Monday after 12 years.

Saturday, 4th October 1952
> Fine day. Stan helped me pick apples. Cleared the Newson Wonder. Yielded about 6 cwts.

Sunday, 5th October 1952
> Glorious day. Started digging in the nursery bed. Went for a walk in the afternoon. Picked sweet corn for dinner – delicious.

Monday, 6th October 1952
Another fine day. Did a bit more digging this evening. Ordered ballast, cement, 2 chimney pots and door from Syneds £5.10.0. Dug first leek.

Tuesday, 7th October 1952
Fine day, rather cold. Mr Milne who has sold his house gave me a lot of flowers, including Christmas Rose. Cookers are falling. Nothing touched by frost yet. Fuschia continues in bloom. Mrs Foster paid off today.

Wednesday, 8th October 1952
Fine day but very misty. Mike is very good. Audrey managed quite well. Terrible train crash at Harrow. Many killed. Planted out the flowers from Mr Milne. Dark at 6.30pm now.

Thursday, 9th October 1952
Another fine day but rain tonight. Bought 2 blue Budgies from Coppuck. Audrey's Mother came up all day. Turfs arrived from Rivetts. Somebody has broken the gate!

Friday, 10th October 1952
Fine sunny day. Mike and David doing well. Mike is strong as a horse. Start my holiday tonight, thank goodness.

Saturday, 11th October 1952
Fine. Stan helped me pick apples again. Went to Wycombe with Audrey and bought her some clothes.

Sunday, 12th October 1952
Fine. Went to Jordans this afternoon to Avoca. Saw the local sectarians playing soft ball on the green. The most model model village I have seen.

Monday, 13th October 1952
Pouring all day. Went to work this morning in response to a telegram from Eddie saying he had a cold. Interview with Mr Davies this afternoon – not very satisfactory but he has agreed to take up my case. Ordered another 50 turfs.

Tuesday, 14th October 1952
Fine. Concreting all day. The old green cock Budgie died today – enteritis I think.

Wednesday, 15th October 1952
Fine. Concreting again. Had a picking of runner beans – I think it is the last (but see on).

Thursday, 16th October 1952
Fine. Mike and I went to the zoo. We had a very nice day. Mike was very interested.

Friday, 17th October 1952
Fine. Odd job day. Picked a bushel or so of apples from the tree by the aviary. Audrey went to Wycombe on her own.

Saturday, 18th October 1952
Fine. Stan helped me once again with the apples. The two large trees at the front are almost clear. Cleared the tree at the back. Moved the deciduous shrubs and planted three Cyprus (Lawsouiana).

Sunday, 19th October 1952
Pouring with rain all day. The Fuschia has finished now except for a few odd blooms. Ordered the following from Waterers: 6 Boskoop Giant, 6 Daniels September, 1 Laxtons Plot (currents), 1 Whinhams Industry, 1 Whitesmith (gooseberries), 1 Dennistons Superb plum (from Cuthberts), 12 Malling Promise. I tried to get Exploit but they haven't got it.

Monday, 20th October 1952
Cold wet day. Heard of the new Pension Scheme – very good. David slept right through last night for the first time.

Tuesday, 21st October 1952
   Dry but very cold. Bought a root of Helleborus Niger and Berberis Thunbergii and Berberis Polyantha from Woolworths. Read in the paper tonight that the Queen is coming to Harrisons on 31st October. Wrote asking for the cesspool to be emptied. My Income Tax refund for Dave is £15.

Saturday, 25th October 1952
   Fine day. Laid some more turfs in the morning. Went to Wycombe in the afternoon – bought Mike an overcoat £3.13.6 and Audrey a pair of shoes 32/-!

Sunday, 26th October 1952
   Fine mild day. Clocks put back last night. Laid all the turfs. Builders arrived at 8am. They completed the chimneys, stopped the leak over the north room. Charged 52/6d. Myrtle and her Mother came on their annual tea visit. Arrived at 3pm left at 9pm!! Nearly all the leaves off the trees. Everywhere is smothered with them and windfall apples. I think the tobacco is developing mildew – blast.

Monday, 27th October 1952
   Damp dull day. Mike went to Audrey's Mother for the day. I bought the rest of the material for the door into Mike's bedroom to be – £1. We shall have spent our Budgie money before we get it. Came home in the dark tonight. Roll on spring.

Tuesday, 28th October 1952
   Wet miserable day. Audrey had a nice picking of runner beans – this must be a record. Audrey re-examined by the doctor and passed out 100%.

Wednesday, 29th October 1952
   Fine pleasant day. I discovered mildew on the midribs of my dried tobacco last weekend so I have stripped all that is dry and put it to ferment in the airing cupboard, to Audrey's disgust. David weighs 10lbs today!!! Audrey's Mother came up all day. Cesspool emptied.

Thursday, 30th October 1952
Dry mild day, turning cold this evening. Brought home plasterboard to make Mike's zoo with. David slept through last night for the second time.

Friday, 31st October 1952
Fine day.

Saturday, 1st November 1952
Rather dull and damp. Swept all the leaves off the grass at the front. Roses arrived. After planting noticed they had sent 2 of 6 sorts instead of 12 different. Paid £1 for a set of zoo animals for Mike.

Sunday, 2nd November 1952
Thoroughly wet, miserable day. Dug the ground for beans and dug up a lot of rhubarb tubers. Builders made the doorway through to Mike's room to be. £4.17.6d. Mike has been most contrary today and has been lucky not to have a hiding. The lawn was covered with leaves again this morning. Most of the trees are completely bare now. The Arctic King sown in August has hearted up nicely. The runner beans are definitely finished.

Monday, 3rd November 1952
Made Mike's zoo this evening.

Wednesday, 5th November 1952
Damp this morning but dry and fine this evening. Aunts Lou and Ethel came to see Audrey and the kids this evening. Gill and Don came this evening and brought a lot of fireworks – we had a smashing display! Mike was pleased, I think.

Thursday, 6th November 1952
Violent wind this evening which blew down a Newton Wonder tree in Mr Walter Jennings' garden. A brother to ours in all probability.

Friday, 7th November 1952
Took 6 Budgies to Jones and Rivetts. Mr Tilley was very pleased with them indeed.

Saturday, 8th November 1952

Fine day. I took Mike into Wycombe and bought him a pair of bootees, Mrs Jefferies' birthday and Christmas presents. Re-roofed the Budgies cage this afternoon.

Sunday, 9th November 1952

Fine morning but dull and damp later. The builders have water-proofed the front bays and this is all we are having done for the time being. Swept all leaves up and we hope the grass will remain clean now. There is a lot of moss to be raked out. Sowed broad beans. Stan and Bridget came for tea. Cut a lettuce Arctic King from the August sowing – nicely hearted. Gave Mr Smith a box of apples and helped him take down the large Cypress tree opposite his lounge.

Monday, 10th November 1952

Dull dry day. The Queen came to Harrisons today. She is very lovely. Audrey and Mike had an invitation and quite a good view. Free drinks all day. Stan got tight and I had to take him to Bill's house to sober him up. Mike got an electric shock. I met the manager of the BFP at lunch and hope to visit the BFP soon. Audrey's Mother and Bill brought us home and stayed for a bit.

Tuesday, 11th November 1952

Fine dry day but very cold. The plot of land bought by Baldwin has been almost cleared and he is stacking building material there.

Wednesday, 12th November 1952

Another fine day and still very cold. Severe frost this morning and lots of birds, mainly Blackbirds, in the garden. I plan to build a feeding tray for them at the weekend.

Thursday, 13th November 1952

Fine again but cold still. Mr McKay came for lunch – gave him some apples. Think Tecome may be a good shrub for the porch. The Christmas Rose Mr Milne gave me is nearly in flower.

Saturday, 15th November 1952
Miserable cold day. Helped Audrey nearly all day getting ready for Mike's party. Ethel sent him a nice cake, a book, some crackers and knife fork and spoon. We gave him the model zoo which pleased him. Terrific bout of cooking all the evening.

Sunday, 16th November 1952
Quite a nice day for the time of the year. Spent the morning in the garden. None of the last lot of Budgie eggs was fertilized. Three cars for Mike's party. 12 for tea. Don wore his new suit. Very successful do. Mike has a lot of presents. A rug for his bedroom and a shirt and tie from his Nan Nan. Trousers and zoo animals from Peg and John. Toy car and book from Gillian and Don etc. Peg and John brought us some plants. We picked two fine bunches of roses from the garden. Must sow Bergamot for the border next year.

Monday, 17th November 1952
Cold damp day. Michael had another present today – a book from Myrtle. David slept through until 5am last night.

Tuesday, 18th November 1952
Hard white frost this morning. David slept through again. Mike seems to have given up sleeping at midday. He listens to the wireless for under fives at 1.45pm with rapt attention.

Wednesday, 19th November 1952
Cold wet miserable day, with teeming rain this evening. The builder's efforts at repairing the roof and bays have evidently been successful. The next job is the porch.

Thursday, 20th November 1952
Sent for 3 kinds of Broom. Audrey ordered 10cwt coal and one bag of coke.

Friday, 21st November 1952
Cold wet and foggy. Went to the Cricket Club dinner with Don and an American friend of his. Heard Lords Carrington and Astor also M P Hall – whom I disliked. Mac and Dick rang up to say they couldn't come on Sunday.

Saturday, 22nd November 1952
Dull and cold. Worked in the garden. Started to clear the bed by the gate. The Christmas Rose is nearly out. Planted out the remaining six roses from Cuthberts. Gill and Don called this evening.

Sunday, 23rd November 1952
A better day. Did a lot of odd jobs in the garden. Pruned the dessert apple Watermans. Planted out a number of home grown shrubs. Don't know what half of them are. Peg and John came for tea and we played cards afterwards.

Monday, 24th November 1952
Very white frost this morning – fine day.

Tuesday, 25th November 1952
Still very cold. Mike has a gastric infection and has been unable to eat anything all day.

Wednesday, 26th November 1952
Mike is better today but Audrey is affected though not so badly. I stayed home this morning and helped with the chores (also planted 3 Broom hybrids in the shrubbery). Audrey is better this evening. It has snowed quite hard and the garden is 1½" deep. Bought 1 cwt potatoes from Howland.

Thursday, 27th November 1952
Still cold. Audrey a lot better but still groggy. Mike was sick again in the night – I think from overeating.

Friday, 28th November 1952

The weather has been too bad for visitors this week. The coldest November for 27 years. We must have used 10 cwts anthracite already and about the same amount of coal.

Saturday, 29th November 1952

Very cold. Spent morning sowing, sawing wood and odd jobbing in the garden. It snowed hard during the afternoon and night. Mike is quite better now. Audrey and I shared part of a bottle of Egg Flip and played cards in the evening.

Sunday, 30th November 1952

Very cold and snow on the ground. Made Mike a snowman and more odd jobs. Audrey's Mother came up and said they wouldn't come for Christmas Day. My Father fetched Mike for tea. I felt as though I had a cold coming.

Monday, 1st December 1952

Bitterly cold day. I took Mike to his Nan Nan's for the day. We had 8 replies for Punch. Chapman, Windermere Widmer End sounds the most promising.

Tuesday, 2nd December 1952

Bitterly cold still. Roads very slippery this morning. I took Punch to Widmer End tonight. A very nice home. He will be a lot better off than here.

Wednesday, 3rd December 1952

Not quite so cold today. A thaw is promised but it hadn't started by this evening.

Thursday, 4th December 1952

Very cold again. Found the missing Budgies this morning. They had got behind the big cage and being unable to open their wings had died. We do have bad luck with our birds.

Friday, 5th December 1952
Very cold still. The staff took Mr Coulton to dinner at the Shillingford Bridge Hotel where there was an extension until midnight – a very excellent meal – wonder how much it will cost. Came home at midday to change – gave Mike a swing in the garden.

Saturday, 6th December 1952
Bitterly cold and foggy. Went to Maidenhead on the train this morning and bought four Budgies. John fetched us in the car for his birthday. Audrey wore a Christmas Rose. The fog was very bad indeed. Three quarters of an hour to get to Wycombe. It had cleared on the way back except at Loudwater where it was quite an adventure.

Sunday, 7th December 1952
Bitterly cold and the fog persists. The AA say the worst they have ever known. Strangely it has been clear and sunny at Flackwell Heath. Stripped the paper off the guest room. An uninspiring job. My Mother came this evening and collected my Pop's birthday present. The windows are very white these mornings. This is the 5th week of cold wintry weather.

Monday, 8th December 1952
Still very cold. Ordered decorating material for the guest bedroom. £3. Plants arrived from Waterers.

Tuesday, 9th December 1952
Milder today, thank goodness – the snow and ice is melting and the roads are filthy. Went to Abbots Kings Langley with Mr Coulton – his car broke down and we had to taxi from Rickmansworth.

Wednesday, 10th December 1952
Very mild and humid today with rain. Mr Burrow and Laurence called this evening – they stayed for ham sandwiches!

Thursday, 11th December 1952

Mild sunny day. Just like spring. Decorating materials arrived and we started working the evening.

Friday, 12th December 1952

Colder today. Took six Budgies to Jones and Rivetts. Arranged to supply him next year – all being well. More decorating this evening.

Saturday, 13th December 1952

Cold and wet but I was able to plant out the fruit bushes although it chose to snow. Mike helped me while Audrey did some Christmas shopping in Wycombe. Took Mike to Harrisons party. It was very good but it was a bit above him. Bought some heavy curtains for the lounge. £5.17.6d plus lining!

Sunday, 14th December 1952

Frosty morning but the sun was quite warm. More decorating – it is almost ready for papering. Brolac paint is good but it stinks. Mac and Dick came up in the afternoon to bring Christmas presents. My Father fetched Mike for tea. He was very pleased with the pullover Audrey made for him.

Monday, 15th December 1952

Woke this morning to find about 2" snow. No buses running down the hill. Came slipping and sliding all over the place. I caught the train into Wycombe. More decorating this evening.

Tuesday, 16th December 1952

The snow is still thick but it is thawing and very slushy. Started to paper in the room.

Wednesday, 17th December 1952

Woke this morning to find not a trace of snow. The weather is quite mild. Unfortunately, some of the paper has bubbled so we have had to strip it off this evening.

Thursday, 18th December 1952
Mild fine day. Audrey's birthday – finished decorating. Audrey's presents included £5 from her Pop. Clock from Peg and John and a nice jumper from Myrtle. I gave her a purse and Mike a bottle of beer!!

Friday, 19th December 1952
Mild and dry with a strong wind. Laid the lino in the bedroom this evening. Gill and Don brought us a Christmas tree, paper chains and Gillian's crib. We spent most of the evening decorating the lounge ready for Christmas and wrapping up presents – bed at midnight.

Saturday, 20th December 1952
Mild with torrential rain during the afternoon and evening. Mike was spellbound with the crib. Audrey's Mother and Father and Peg and John came for the birthday tea (ham and mince pies etc). It was a very pleasant evening and we played the usual games. I went Christmas shopping this morning and the shops are crowded and most of the best things sold. 1cwt coke delivered. Ordered 5cwt anthracite.

Sunday, 21st December 1952
Beautiful spring-like day. Rose at 9am. Helped Audrey clear up. Went into the garden and planted out the shrubs that came this week: Rhus Cotinus, Cotoneaster Franchetii, Hibiscus Syriacus, Ceanothus Veitchianus, Tecoma Radicans. Also cut down part of the apple tree by the back bedroom and sawed a few Christmas logs. Mike fell off the step ladder into a bowl of muddy water. Spent the evening working out the accounts and find that we are about £18 in debt! No visitors today, thank heavens.

Monday, 22nd December 1952
Mild damp foggy and miserable. My Mother came up with presents for all. Mike now has 3 elephants. Started to make the curtains but it is a big job. Mike's tricycle is being delivered to Milnes. David laughed out loud for the first time. He is a very good baby and hardly cries at all. He now sleeps through to between 6.30 and 7.30am.

Tuesday, 23rd December 1952
Finished the curtains today, after a great struggle during which the machine broke on the last lap.

Wednesday, 24th December 1952
Mild and fine. Finished work early and caught the 3.30 pm bus home. Lunch with Eddie at the Red Lion. Audrey's Mother and Father, Gill and Don and Peggy and John came along this evening with the presents. Packed Mike's pillowcase and stocking and wheeled his tricycle in. Put a mince pie on the hall table for Father Christmas.

Thursday, 25th December 1952
Beautiful spring-like morning, but torrential rain in the afternoon and evening. Mike woke early and took his presents and Father Christmas as a matter of course. Beautiful dinner. Drinking and eating all day. My Mother and Father and Gill and Don came up for an hour this evening. Olive stayed at Loudwater with a bad throat.

Friday, 26th December 1952
Dull damp day. No visitors. Lots to eat. We had a super chicken from Jennings. Took Mike out on his bike this afternoon. He can't peddle yet. Picked a vase of Christmas Roses.

Saturday, 27th December 1952
Very foggy and damp. Pruned the large Bramley with my new long handled secateurs. Cut out an enormous amount of unwanted wood. Hope the fruit will be larger next year. Audrey's Mother and Father came up for an hour in the afternoon.

Sunday, 28th December 1952
Extremely white frost – the fog has disappeared. Not a bad morning. Cleared more grass from the bed by the gate. Beef for dinner today. Disappointed it wasn't pork. Mike went to his Nan Nan's for tea. A very quiet but very enjoyable Christmas. The white Hyacinths were in flower. Noticed that a bud is visible on the Hyacinth planted outdoors.

Monday, 29th December 1952
Dull damp and cold day. Mike went to Audrey's Mother while Audrey cleaned up the Christmas debacle. Very busy at work. Chimney on fire in the lounge. Bags of panic. Had to put the fire out quickly.

Tuesday, 30th December 1952
Foggy damp and miserable. Bedroom very damp. No eggs this week. According to the papers this is the coldest autumn for 33 years.

Wednesday, 31st December 1952
Torrential rain first thing this morning, dark and miserable – roll on spring. David is still very good and very rarely cries. He sits on the chair or settee for an hour or more just watching. Mike is almost able to ride his bike properly.

Thursday, 1st January 1953
Cold – damp and snow. Audrey bilious in the night – missed the bus. Expecting the sweep. A shocking start to the New Year.

Friday, 2nd January 1953
Cold bright day. Sweep came. Mr Lane. Only charged 2/6d. Arranged with Mr Carter of Le Merle for David's Christening. Had a drink with Mr Baker and gave him an enquiry.

Saturday, 3rd January 1953
Cold. Snow showers and bright periods. Audrey went into Wycombe while I held fort in the morning. Started digging round the currant bushes where I found the back door key. Mike lost it about a year ago. Don came up for the evening while Gill and her Mother went to a show. He had received a nasty blow while playing rugby and was afraid he might have broken his nose.

Sunday, 4th January 1953
Milder – dull. More digging. The broad beans aren't up but I dug one up and it was growing well and even showing green. Mike had a little ride on his bike. He is gradually learning. My Mother came up in the evening and took some apples.

Monday, 5th January 1953
Very cold day. Mike went to his Nan Nan's. She bought him a duster for his bike and he went to sleep coming home in the bus. Audrey washed her hair. Wrote for the cesspool to be emptied.

Tuesday, 6th January 1953
Woke to find about 5 inches of snow. Thawing during the day with consequent slush. Had a hair cut.

Wednesday, 7th January 1953
Snow is still in the garden but has mostly cleared in the town. Very cold all day.

Thursday, 8th January 1953
Cold damp weather. The snow is still thick in the garden. Guy Lisle came up for the evening.

Friday, 9th January 1953
Cold damp and foggy. Mr Coulton brought me home in his car. Gill and Don spent the evening with us. Don's nose is better. Mike hasn't been in the garden to play for ages. Drat this weather.

Saturday, 10th January 1953
Milder and the snow disappeared today. Bit more digging in the garden. Took Mike into Wycombe and bought some marbles. Have got a lousy cold. Hope nobody else catches it. Ordered 4cwt coal and 1cwt coke. Paid for coke.

Sunday, 11th January 1953
Dull damp day. Odd job in the garden. Mike can't ride his bike on the rough paths very well yet. My cold is lousy. Planted the Christmas tree that Gill and Don gave us.

Monday, 12th January 1953
Dull and cold but we saw the sun. Last night the cows came into the garden and did a lot of damage to the plants. Ate the buds off the Rhododendrons and the Wallflowers. Mr Jennings says they aren't his cows! My cold has been shocking today. Left work early.

Tuesday, 13th January 1953
Dull and cold, damp and foggy. A beastly day. Gerald Smith (whose cows they were) says he will come to see me on Sunday to settle the damages. Mike seems to have caught my cold, also Audrey – slightly.

Wednesday, 14th January 1953
Damp and foggy with heavy condensation. Mike's cold is very heavy. George Jennings came round and offered to pay all damages.

Thursday, Wednesday, 15th January 1953
Damp and foggy with excessive condensation. The bedroom walls are literally wet. Audrey went to the doctor with piles. Bridget had her baby – boy 7¼ lbs. Mike's cold is getter better. Cesspool emptied. Wrote for two jobs in The Telegraph.

Friday, 16th January 1953
Better weather today but still damp.

Saturday, 17th January 1953
Mild and damp, the fog has almost gone. Did a few odd jobs and wood chopping. The broad beans aren't up yet. Audrey took Mike into the town in the afternoon. Dick and Ben came up in the evening and we had a few 'Rockets' at the Green Man. Presented Jennings with a bill for £5.

Sunday, 18th January 1953
Beautiful spring-like day. Feels good to be alive after all this beastly wet and fog. Gerald Smith has offered to supply flowering shrubs in lieu of cash for the damages. I accepted. Lots of visitors. Mike to his Nan Nan's for tea. The apples are going down but there are still a lot. No market for them at present.

Monday, 19th January 1953
Cold and foggy again. Can't see the kitchen walls for washing tonight. David has a runny left eye.

Tuesday, 20th January 1953
　　Cold day but sunny at Flackwell – beautiful hoar frost first thing. David's eye seems quite better. Mike's cold and my cold seem better and Audrey's piles are OK so long as she takes her medicine. The place is rather like a hospital. Ordered my seeds from Waterers tonight.

Wednesday, 21st January 1953
　　Damp and cold but the fog has cleared. Audrey's Mother and Father came up this evening to discuss holidays. We are booking Sandpiper for a fortnight starting 11th July. We also spoke about the job that Bill has been offered. Gillian's yellow Budgie was gassed after laying 2 eggs.

Thursday, 22nd January 1953
　　Damp cold day again. I am very busy and fed up at work. Wrote for another job. Gillian and Don came up this evening and had a free bath. Brought the blue cock Budgie to go in the aviary. 4 cwts coal arrived. No more ration left.

Friday, 23rd January 1953
　　Damp and cold – turning very cold at night. Mick King cured some of my tobacco and it smells very good. I gave him some apples which pleased us both.

Saturday, 24th January 1953
　　Damp and very cold all day. Too cold for me to pluck up courage to go into the garden even. Bill's birthday. Bought him the Winter Country Man and ordered the next 3 editions. Chicken for tea. It was very nice indeed. David and Mike both very good. John drove us home in a snow storm.

Sunday, 25th January 1953
　　Another fine Sunday. Sunshine nearly all day. Cut and trimmed Jennings' hedge at the front and sundry odd jobs. Mike went for a walk with Neil in the morning and played with Gillian and Frances in the afternoon.

Monday, 26th January 1953

Fine and sunny but rather cold. Took Mike to Benjamin Road but had to bring him back because Bill was in bed with flu. Dick called in the morning with a safety strap for David.

Tuesday, 27th January 1953

Wet windy and milder. Mike seems a bit hot and cold today – afraid he may have a chill. David's eye was discharging this morning and Audrey noticed a foreign body which may have caused the trouble. RMT is away this week which makes life harder.

Wednesday, 28th January 1953

Fairly mild and sunny. Mike has a temperature of 103° – flu we think. Dr Wright came. He also looked at David's eye. I don't know if he saw Audrey's bottom. Mike slept nearly all the morning but seemed no worse this evening.

Thursday, 29th January 1953

Fine warm day. Mike seems a lot better but he still has a temperature this evening of 101.5°. Bill is still supposed to be in bed. Audrey's Mother came this afternoon and brought Mike a chicken and some Daffodils. Picked a small vase of Winter Aconite.

Friday, 30th January 1953

Wet mild and windy. Mike's temperature 101° this morning. He slept most of the day. But he had a good tea (chicken) and his temperature normal tonight. The doctor hasn't been. John is in bed with a cold. Gill and Don came up and Gill is not too well.

Saturday, 31st January 1953

Cold and damp and gales. The Northern Ireland Car Ferry Steamer sank in rough seas with loss of 133 lives. Mike's temperature is OK today and he got up after dinner. He is not eating a lot yet. The doctor has not been again. Purged the mice in the aviary and killed six this evening.

Sunday, 1st February 1953

Bright sunny day with a gale blowing. The east coast flooded with terrible destruction and the loss of many lives. Mike stayed in bed until dinner time. He has a nasty cough. Bill came up this morning to report. Mrs Jeffries ill in bed again and Audrey's Mother not too well. Did odd jobs about the house and started to make the asparagus bed. The clothes certainly 'frackled' on the line.

Monday, 2nd February 1953

Sunny day with cold wind. Mike played in his bedroom in the morning. He has a very poor appetite.

Tuesday, 3rd February 1953

Very cold day – dry but rather dull. Mike is still without much of an appetite.

Wednesday, 4th February 1953

Very cold day. Mike is much better today and has had a better appetite. He is having his breakfasts in bed these days. David remains very well as do Audrey and I – except for being cold, tired and fed up. Roll on spring. 1 cwt coke arrived today. We have been out of boiler fuel for about a week so it is very welcome. I saw Mr Carter tonight and provisionally arranged the Christening for 22nd February at 4pm.

Thursday, 5th February 1953

A cold day again. David can almost sit up unaided. He never seems to cry which suits us.

Friday, 6th February 1953

Very cold day. Audrey and family went to Wycombe. Her Father fetched her and took her back at tea time. Gill and Don came to see us this evening. Mike's appetite is back and he is trying to catch up on lost time.

Saturday, 7th February 1953
Very cold day with severe frost. David's eye very runny and appears to have a scratch on it. Called the doctor who prescribed drops and Penicillin ointment. Went to see Wycome and Romford (0–5). Shocking display. Don and Gillian stayed the evening. We played at séances – Don was much impressed.

Sunday, 8th February 1953
Bitterly cold with intense frost followed by snow after dinner. Pipes frozen in the small bedroom for the first time this winter. David's eye seems OK now. No work at all in the garden this weekend.

Monday, 9th February 1953
Frozen snow this morning. No buses running down the hill.

Tuesday, 10th February 1953
Shocking wet day. The gaps in the sea walls on the coast have not yet been closed and there is danger of further flooding next week.

Wednesday, 11th February 1953
Cold wet snow. Gales and snow all over the country. Flood warnings on the coast. The snow in the north is the worst for many years. 9 foot drifts. 40 main roads are blocked according to the wireless. The snow is only very slight here at the moment though the forecast is bad. We look with dismay at our diminishing coal supplies.

Thursday, 12th February 1953
Snow showers all day. Drifts 30 foot deep in the Peak District of Derby. The ground is covered here but it is only an inch or two deep. Mrs Seymour came round collecting for the Flood Relief Fund. The country has appealed to Europe for 10 million sandbags to build sea walls.

Friday, 13th February 1953
Cold and sunny.

Saturday, 14th February 1953

Woke to find about 6 inches of snow. It was a very still morning and the snow was a lovely sight; every branch and twig of the trees was loaded. I went into Wycombe and bought some Silecine plastic coating for the hall ceiling and started work on it in the afternoon. Gill and Don and my father came up this evening. Gill and Don stayed late and we had a séance to forecast the treble chance! The snow has been thawing on and off and quite a lot has gone. Had to give the ceiling another coat. Gill and Don came for tea and brought back the electric fire they borrowed. Audrey did not feed David at 10pm last night and he slept through until about 4am.

Monday, 16th February 1953

Cold and fine. Started painting the woodwork in the hall so that we can paper tomorrow.

Tuesday, 17th February 1953 (Shrove Tuesday)

Mild and wet. The snow has gone, thank goodness. Papered part of the hall tonight.

Wednesday, 18th February 1953 (Shrove Wednesday)

Fine mid day. It is quite light when I leave work but dark by the time I get home. The Christening has been fixed for 5pm Sunday. David has been off his food today. He has slept through from 6pm until 6am the last two nights. Finished papering the main hall. The paper looks nice. 5cwt anthracite delivered today.

Thursday, 19th February 1953

Mild and damp. Almost light enough to look round the garden. David continues to sleep through.

Friday, 20th February 1953

Mild and dry with strong breeze. David all the afternoon with a chopper. Audrey in a sweat! We think he is cutting a tooth. Undercoated the front and back doors this evening using Brolac 'cream'. One or two Delphiniums sprouting.

Saturday, 21st February 1953
Dull and mild. Depressing day. The garden looks awful. Murrays let us down over the carpet so Audrey went into Wycombe and got the money back. Dug a bit more of the asparagus bed. Audrey spent the afternoon making cakes. Put the boxes in for the birds. We have got one pair in a separate cage to mate.

Sunday, 22nd February 1953
Better day today. David cried at the Christening when the hymn was sung. The tea and games afterwards went off well. David had some nice presents.

Monday, 24th February 1953
Mild and sunny. Michael went to Audrey's Mother while Audrey cleaned up the debris. Michael has a new pair of shoes and a haircut today. He's doing well.

Tuesday, 25th February 1953
Mild and sunny again. Some of the flowers are shooting up and the Polyanthus are trying to flower. Did some painting in the hall this evening. It is a long job.

Wednesday, 25th February 1953
Another fine day. David sat up in his pram unaided for an hour today. I ordered 14lbs of bird seed from Jones & Rivetts today. More painting this evening. David continues to sleep through until about 6.30am.

Thursday, 26th February 1953
Fine day. Very busy at work. Not much decorating this evening. Audrey has started weeding the front beds. We have a mouse in the kitchen – it woke Audrey up three times gnawing at something!

Friday, 27th February 1953
Best day of the year so far. Audrey went to her Mother's for the day. We all caught the train. David and I rode in the guard's van. Audrey bought a BMK carpet and rugs to match from Ladymans. We spent the evening shifting furniture to fit it.

Saturday, 28th February 1953
Dull first thing but fine and sunny later. The wind has gone to the north and it is colder. Decorating all the morning and part of the afternoon. Audrey did some weeding after dinner and I pruned the rose trees. The herbaceous plants are coming through and I have applied slug killer liberally.

Sunday, 1st March 1953
Cold and misty first thing but sunshine for the rest of the day. Nearly finished the asparagus bed. Discovered rats in the rubbish dump and a Blue Tit building in a rainwater pipe. No visitors whatever this weekend.

Monday, 2nd March 1953
Cold and foggy with sun during the day. Decorating this evening interrupted by Gillian and Don. Put sticky traps down for the mice who seem to have gone for a holiday tonight.

Tuesday, 3rd March 1953
Sunny day. Received 7 shrubs from Gerald Smith. Painting in the hall tonight.

Wednesday, 4th March 1953
Fine and sunny. More painting. Audrey's Mother came up. It was very warm in the afternoon and Mike did some sunbathing.

Thursday, 5th March 1953
Fine day again but the mornings have been very cold this week. Mike had a bilious attack this evening but it doesn't seem to have upset him much. No decorating tonight.

Friday, 6th March 1953
Fine and not quite so cold. Completed the paper hanging tonight. Only 4 more doors to paint.

Saturday, 7th March 1953
Fine day after a dull start. I took Mike into Wycombe this morning, called at Dick's and collected the baby chair. Spent the afternoon weeding at the front. Planted out the shrubs from Smith. Audrey's Mother and Father came to tea and stayed the evening. Bill helped with the rat hunt which was unsuccessful. He is still wavering about his job.

Sunday, 8th March 1953
Beautiful fine day. Audrey bilious all day. She felt like nothing on earth. Fortunately my Father collected Mike in the afternoon. Sowed brussels, January King white and purple sprouting, leeks, broccoli Walcheren.

Monday, 9th March 1953
Fine sunny day. Audrey seems much better but I have felt rotten and have had practically nothing to eat. We think we have been stuffing too much. Mike spent the day at his Nan Nan's and went to sleep on the bus as usual. 1cwt coke and 1cwt nutty slack arrived.

Tuesday, 10th March 1953
Dry but rather dull. Everybody well again today, thank goodness. Did some painting this evening. The mornings are still very cold.

Wednesday, 11th March 1953
Dry and dull again. Bill gave his notice today. No decorating this evening. Audrey's Mother came up this afternoon. There are eggs in the boxes of the 3 pairs in the aviary. We hope to release the 4th pair soon. I am to be paid monthly by cheque as from 3rd April.

Thursday, 12th March 1953
Dull and damp, rather cold but still no rain. Mac came up for the day and Dick came for a meal in the evening. Suzanne walks very well for 15 months. She has 4 teeth and says 'da da' and 'ta'. She wouldn't have much to do with Mike.

Friday, 13th March 1953
Similar day to yesterday. We did some painting this evening. I wrote to Jones & Rivetts and offered them up to 50 Budgies. Mike has a discharge from his left eye.

Saturday, 14th March 1953
Cloudy and cold at first but fine later. Mike's eye seems better today. Visited Mr Baker to get some Montbretia. Spent the afternoon cleaning up the shed and garden. Had a real striking bonfire. More painting this evening, only 1½ doors to do!

Sunday, 15th March 1953
Fine sunny day but rather a cold wind. Mike's eye has been queer again after dinner. One or two Daffodils out. Sowed lettuce, beet, parsnip, onions and Clarkia and Anchusa. Get Oxalis Deppes.

Monday, 16th March 1953
Fine and dry. Took Mike to his Nan Nan's. He is not quite himself but his eye seems better.

Tuesday, 17th March 1953
Dry. Painting this evening. Michael spent the morning lying in the very warm sun. It seems to have done him good.

Wednesday, 18th March 1953
Dry. Michael seems quite himself again today. David is getting quite brown with all this sun. He can almost crawl.

Thursday, 19th March 1953
Dry. Terrific panic this morning. No breakfast. Went to Unwins of Woking with YMPs. Gillian and Don and my Mother visited us this evening.

Friday, 20th March 1953
Dry. Finished the painting tonight. Thank heavens! David had wind tonight and was awake all the evening.

Saturday, 21st March 1953
Fine and dry but very cold first thing (a few choppers about). I creosoted the west side of the house. Audrey and I went to Reading with Don and my Mother while Gill minded the children. We saw Reading beat Bristol Rovers 2-0. Their first league defeat since September. First day of spring. Hurrah!

Sunday, 22nd March 1953

Fine dry day again. Planted out the asparagus bed: 36 plants in an area 6' x 15'. Mike was fetched by Audrey's Father at 11.30am for the day. Saw a Tortoise Shell butterfly. We very badly need some rain. Pickled some eggs in water glass – thinking of next winter already. No seeds up yet.

Monday, 23rd March 1953

Dry hot and sunny. Mike stayed at home and played in the garden all day – Audrey hardly saw him. Wrote for the cesspool to be emptied.

Tuesday, 24th March 1953

Dry but dull and oppressive. Queen Mary died this evening.

Wednesday, 25th March 1953

Dry warm and sunny. The hedges are just coming into leaf and the Daffodils are full out in the garden. I was able to do some weeding in the evening until about 10 to 7. Lunch with Mr Minoros of Bowaters.

Thursday, 26th March 1953

Bright morning but rain this afternoon – very welcome – the first since 19th February! Up at 6 this morning, did some weeding before going to work. Audrey spring cleaned Mike's room including the cupboards. My Mother came up this evening for a basket of apples. 3 Budgies hatched out.

Friday, 27th March 1953

Dry and sunny but rather cold. We all went to Wycombe on the train this morning and Bill brought us back in the car. The larch trees are a haze of green. The cherry buds are green and about to open.

Saturday, 28th March 1953

Dull and cold. Audrey took Mike into the town in the morning while I cleaned up a few tools. Planted out some autumn sown Brussels plants and two Lawson Cyprus. Gill and Don bought up 8 shrubs and a yellow fancy Carnation from the Ideal Home Exhibition.

Sunday, 29th March 1953

Dull wet day. Planted out the shrubs but no other gardening. Stan came for tea – Bridget is at Ipswich. Mike and Dave have both developed colds. There has been a gale blowing all day and the trees wave about alarmingly.

Monday, 30th March 1953

Bright cold day with torrential showers. Still very windy. March is certainly going out like a lion.

Tuesday, 31st March 1953

Bright cold and windy. The outer cases of the cherry are open – a week earlier than last year. It may mean the frost will catch it. There is a pair of Long Tailed Tits about the garden. Must look out for a nest. The boys' colds are a bit better today. The old green hen is ill again. Put her in the small cage and put her 5 eggs under the others.

Wednesday, 1st April 1953

Nobody caught anybody – aren't we slow!

Thursday, 2nd April 1953

Wet day. Got soaked coming home this evening. Doesn't look like being much of a holiday.

Friday, 3rd April 1953 (Good Friday)

Fine sunny day despite the weather forecast. We concentrated on weeding in the flower beds. The herbaceous plants are all making fine growth. Gillian and Don came up this evening – we played the usual games and got to bed at 1am.

Saturday, 4th April 1953

Another fine day. More weeding. Put weed killer on the paths. Sowed Canary Creeper, Allwoodii, Violas, Lychnis, Gallandia, lettuce, beet and kohl rabi. Re-sowed vegetables as slugs have had them again this year. Mike went out for the day with Audrey's Mother and Father. Peg and John came up this evening – we played marbles!

Sunday, 5th April 1953 (Easter Day)
   Wet and rather miserable. It cleared up enough in the afternoon to take Mike for a ride on his tricycle. My Mother came for tea. Mike has had lots of Easter eggs. Went to Loudwater and did a bit of painting for my Father.

Monday, 6th April 1953 (Easter Monday)
   Another wet day. Mike found a baby rabbit which I caught and made a hutch for. Thinned out the plum and damson tree at the bottom of the garden. There isn't much fruit blossom this year, although the cherry tree has a lot of buds. We all had a walk round the village this afternoon. No visitors.

Tuesday, 7th April 1953
   Bright sunny day in contrast to yesterday. Very busy at work. The flowering currant by the bedroom is dying. Did a little bit of weeding in the garden and started a compost heap. Received electric light bill for £7 plus £10 final repayment on cooker.

Wednesday, 8th April 1953
   Bright and sunny but cold wind with a sharp frost first thing. The very first of the cherry blossom is out. Arranged for a demonstration of an Atco motor mower and an Ajax on Saturday. The grass needs cutting very much.

Thursday, 9th April 1953
   Dull with a very cold north wind. Too cold to work in the garden this evening and too dark by 7 o'clock. Mike full of high spirits. His speech is definitely becoming more distinct. The rabbit is still. David is just beginning to cut his first tooth.

Friday, 10th April 1953
   Fine day. Audrey did a lot of cooking for my birthday tea. It appears that we shall get 8 Budgies only from the first hatching.

Saturday, 11th April 1953

Fine day but a cold wind. Started cutting some of the grass. Lords hardware shop demonstration. Atco motor mower. Very good! Very nice birthday tea. Audrey's Mother and Father, Peg and John only. But Gill and Don and Mac, Dick and Ben called. We rose at 5.45am and dug and hoed in the garden.

Sunday, 12th April 1953

Shocking wet day. Children quite good. I went to Loudwater and helped my Father with a bit of painting. No gardening – the garden is getting rather behind this year. David's tooth is just through.

Monday, 13th April 1953

Fine windy day, rather cold. Mike to his Nan Nan's. Audrey made a tremendous effort and cut nearly all the grass. I did a bit of edge trimming in the evening.

Tuesday, 14th April 1953

Bright periods with very cold wind. It even hailed. The cherry blossom is full out and the plum and damson nearly so. One of the fledgling Budgies seems to be half blue and half green. Too cold for gardening tonight. The seeds are not doing very well.

Wednesday, 15th April 1953

Sunny but still cold. Lunch with McNay who invited us to see Coronation decorations in June. Collected a hen from Coppuck and walked home through the fields – scraggy looking bird. Dug a couple of rows. Mike left the rabbit's cage open and it had gone this morning. Apparently our yellow Daisies will do well in the shade under trees! They are called Doronicum.

Thursday, 16th April 1953

Sunny and milder. Audrey did some more grass cutting. Mike has been invited to Frances' birthday party. We bought her a Bumble book. One of the young Budgies has died leaving 7. Very poor first hatching.

Friday, 17th April 1953
   Milder but wet. Mike gave Frances her book first thing this morning. He came back from the party tonight very red in the face and tired out.

Saturday, 18th April 1953
   Dull and wet at first but it soon cleared up and turned out a nice day. Started preparing for more grass at the back. My Mother came up in the afternoon and took some apples. They are mostly bad now. Gill and Don came for the evening. We went to The George at Marlow while Gill minded the kids. Mike woke up and wanted a drink of water!

Sunday, 19th April 1953
   Fine warm day but a chilly wind nevertheless. Mr Baker brought me some fine lettuce plants. My early taters are up. Have strawed 2 rows. We went for a walk round and had a long monologue from old Mr Howard.

Monday, 20th April 1953
   Beautiful sunny day. Very warm indeed. Mike went to his Nan Nan's. Gave the new lawn mower a good try out. It cuts beautifully. The pear blossom is just passing white bud. Lime sulphur sprayed the pears. Audrey heard the cuckoo.

Tuesday, 21st April 1953
   Beautiful summer-like day. Best of the year. Dave has got 2 teeth. Mike found some paint and proceeded to paint the greenhouse. He was covered from head to foot. Cut some more grass this evening. It is full of weeds – must get some Verdone. Pickled another 12 eggs. Cherry blossom past its best. Audrey visited Mrs Baker.

Wednesday, 22nd April 1953
   Another hot sunny day. Peggy fainted and everyone rather worried. I came home at lunch unexpectedly. It was very pleasant. Finished cutting the grass at the front. Cesspool emptied. Must grow perpetual strawberries – La Sans Rivale sounds one of the best.

Thursday, 23rd April 1953
Hot and sunny. Audrey went to the dentist. 5 teeth to be filled. Went for a drink with Audrey and her Mum and Pop this evening while Gill and Don minded the kids. No gardening this evening except to set a few seeds of Anchusa.

Friday, 24th April 1953
Warm day but not so sunny. The seeds of various things are not doing so well, although two rows of lettuce up. We could do with a few showers. Spent the evening blocking up the holes in Smith's garage. Started to clear the mess up by the greenhouse. It is rather dangerous for Mike. Audrey has sorted most of the apples. There are still about 3 boxes full.

Saturday, 25th April 1953
Fine sunny day. Audrey went into Wycombe while Mike played in the garden with 6 or 7 kids. Cleaned up generally and made some cloches in the morning. Went to Audrey's Mum's birthday party in the afternoon. Very nice tea – chicken. Chunky (Peggy's dog) was alleged to have peed on the Pansies. Mac and Dick came up for the evening.

Sunday, 26th April 1953
Another sunny day but a cold wind. Worked in the garden all day. Re-sowed Brussels and Savoys! Sowed sweet corn. The cherry tree is nearly over blooming. The Flowering Cherry is approaching its best. Mike played with Frances all day. We all dashed off to see the decorating at my Mother's house this evening.

Monday, 27th April 1953
Rain and rather cold. It should do the garden good. Took Mrs Baker some apples tonight. Mike went to his Nan Nan's. Slept soundly on the bus as usual. He has some new sandals from Woolworths – they seem very good.

Tuesday, 28th April 1953
Cold and showery with bright periods. Started to paint the window in the front room. Too damp and miserable for gardening. Had a very nice dinner at Audrey's Mothers: pork and stuffing followed by trifle and ice cream.

Wednesday, 29th April 1953
Still cold and wet. Audrey's Mother came up this afternoon. Audrey is doing spring cleaning these days. Wrote enquiring the cost of making up loose covers. Planted Chrysanths for Audrey's Mother.

Thursday, 30th April 1953
Poured all last night and all day. Stopped for an hour this evening and we put in plants: Sweet Rocket white and purple – Erigeron Quakerness, Aster Subcaeruleus Mauve (orange centre), Rudbeckia Purpurea (purple with dark centre) from B Lake, Redgate Hill Nurseries, Heacham, Kings Lynn – strawberry specialist. Rain coming through the bay continuously. Blast! We have christened David 'Piggy' – he will eat anything. Received my cheque, thank goodness. Still in debt though.

Friday, 1st May 1953
Cold wet and thoroughly miserable. A poor start for May. Too cold to go into the garden. Painted the window instead.

Saturday, 2nd May 1953
Fine warm day, at last. Audrey went into the town in the morning. Spent the day gardening. Listened to the Cup Final. Matthews got his cup medal. Audrey's Mother and Father called in the evening and brought my watch. The Flowering Cherry is full out. Sowed the grass at the back.

Sunday, 3rd May 1953
Glorious sunny day. Audrey wore a summer's dress for the first time this year. Cut the grass this morning and had the rest of the day off. David spends the afternoons being amused these days. A comet crashed today, no survivors. All Budgies out from the hatching.

Monday, 4th May 1953
Rather dull and cool today. Audrey did some weeding while I sowed swedes and another lot of lettuce. David can't crawl yet but he is starting to stand up in his pram. Mike is constantly picking flowers and giving them to Smiths next door.

Tuesday, 5th May 1953
Fine hot day. Started to make the aviary for the young birds. No gardening but the grass is growing like mad. The front gate is literally falling to pieces – one panel has completely fallen out.

Wednesday, 6th May 1953
Fine sunny day, very close. I have a cold coming – my usual I suppose – blast! Gill and Don came up this evening and we went to see a bungalow for sale at Hazelmere – not very impressive. Doronicum almost over. Cherianthus just coming into flower. Aubretia is well past its best. The B Darwinii is full out. The Apple Blossom is full out – rather later than last year. There is virtually none on the trees at the front except the Codling which is loaded.

Thursday, 7th May 1953
Fine and sunny but with a rather cold wind. We spent the evening making the aviary, it is shaping quite well. Audrey hoed most of the flower beds this afternoon. We put Verdone on parts of the grass last week and the results are very evident already. The Flowering Cherry is beginning to lose its blossom.

Friday, 8th May 1953
Fine and sunny. I went to a sausage supper at the Cricket Club with Don. Norman Plumridge sang some catchy old songs. Quite enjoyable.

Saturday, 9th May 1953
Fine and sunny. Worked on the aviary all day, it is virtually finished. We have 11 eggs in 3 boxes so far. The Flowering Cherry is beginning to lose its blossom. Audrey cut the grass at the front. The broad beans are well in flower.

Sunday, 10th May 1953
Fine and sunny with a cold wind. Worked in the garden all the morning and had the afternoon off. Set runner beans. Went with Gill and Don to see a house at Cock Lane – no go!

Monday, 11th May 1953
Fine and warm. David can stand up in his pram without holding but he can't crawl yet. A white frost this morning but no damage done. The early potatoes are about 1 foot high. Mike went to his Nan Nan's and fell asleep as usual coming home.

Tuesday, 12th May 1953
Fine still. Gill and Don got their Anglia today. They took us for a drink to the Riviera Hotel at Maidenhead to celebrate, while my Mother baby sat.

Wednesday, 13th May 1953
Fine. David has almost got his second pair of teeth. He is a tremendous eater and seems to be always yelling for more. Audrey cut the grass at the back this afternoon and helped me work in the vegetable patch this evening. We had a big bonfire, sticked the peas. I have still quite a lot of digging to do. The vegetable seeds have been rather unsuccessful this year though there will be a few plants.

Thursday, 14th May 1953
Rain last night and today at last. Audrey went to the dentist today and had 2 temporary fillings. Nan Nan minded the children. Finished the bird aviary tonight. Hope to put the birds in tomorrow. We have 17 eggs in 4 boxes.

Friday, 15th May 1953
Wet day. Audrey went to the dentist again – 1 filled. Gill and Don came up in the evening to thank us for Gill's birthday blouse. She has had her hair cut short – it looks very nice.

Saturday, 16th May 1953
Wet, windy and sunny intervals. Not a very nice day. Finished off the aviary. The 7 birds look rather lonely. Myrtle came for tea. The broad beans are rather beaten down with the rain.

Sunday, 17th May 1953
   Terribly windy and wet with torrential rain at times. I had the trots. Spent the morning in bed and felt lousy. All the visitors under the sun this afternoon.

Monday, 18th May 1953
   Dull and wet with a slight frost this morning. The garden is getting out of hand. I intended to work like mad this evening but it simply poured. The Broom is just coming out (later this year). The tomatoes under the cloches are beginning to flower. The Peony buds are just breaking.

Tuesday, 19th May 1953
   Dull and damp. Worked in the garden this evening. Sowed main crop peas, Cherianthus, Wallflowers, Canterbury Bells (cup and saucer), Sweet Williams and Biennial Foxgloves, Suttons Excelsior hybrids.

Wednesday, 20th May 1953
   Fine warm day. Close this evening. Cut the front lawn including the long grass and started cutting the front privet hedge – I hope to cut the hawthorn hedge at the weekend. David is cutting 3 teeth at once. 2 birds hatched out today.

Thursday, 21st May 1953
   Fine day. Michael has a sore throat and doesn't feel too well. Gill and Don called this evening and we set them to gardening. Don scythed down a lot of undergrowth.

Friday, 22nd May 1953
   Fine and showery. Michael's throat is quite sore and he has a temperature of 103°. The doctor is calling in the morning.

Saturday, 23rd May 1953
   Fine day – very close and muggy. Michael has tonsillitis. The doctor has prescribed M&B. Audrey has broken the thermometer! Spent the day cutting the front hedges. Just the tops left to trim. Peg and John called and brought Mike some cherries and books.

Sunday, 24th May 1953 (Whit Sunday)
Scorching day. Mike got up for dinner and we all had our tea in the garden. Audrey went to Cookham in the car in the evening and got my melon plants. My Father came up to say my Mother has to go into hospital on Tuesday.

Monday, 25th May 1953 (Whit Monday)
Another scorcher. Had to go to work because we are having the Monday off before the Coronation. Sweated like a pig in the garden this evening digging and weeding. Michael is much better, thank goodness. The runner beans are up.

Tuesday, 26th May 1953
Fine but much cooler. Went to Aylesbury to see Coppuck in hospital. Arrived back late to find my Father and Gill at home. They are going to watch the Coronation while I mind the kids. Mike is OK today. The Ceanothus is in flower.

Wednesday, 27th May 1953
Wet day. Mike is OK now. Planted out Brussels and January King. Went to Loudwater tonight. My Mother had the operation on her bunion – everything OK. I am going to see her Saturday evening. Gill and Don's furniture went today. Pinched out tops of broad beans.

Thursday, 28th May 1953
Dry and sunny today. Spent the whole evening cutting the grass really short. Only did half the front lawn. The spikes of Rye grass have been very troublesome. Audrey had a terrific bonfire burning hedge chippings etc. Mike is very keen on his new room.

Friday, 29th May 1953
Fine day. Audrey's Mum and Pop came up this evening and lent Audrey some money to get a dress as my cheque hasn't arrived. Gill and Don also arrived and Bill, Don and I went to the local. Grass cutting earlier this evening.

Saturday, 30th May 1953

Another fine day. Audrey bought a dress, hat, gloves, stockings and underwear. We went into Wycombe by train, pram and all. Gillian came for tea. Spent the afternoon cutting grass. The front looks its best ever: Lupins, Pinks and Catmint out. Went to see my Mother this evening. She looks well but rather fed up at being in bed and missing the Coronation.

Sunday, 31st May 1953

Fine but a very cold wind. Rentokiled Mike's room and put his furniture in. He moved in this evening. We went for a walk round the village this afternoon. The pigeons are eating the cabbage and brussels plants wholesale.

Monday, 1st June 1953

Cold and wet. I went into Wycombe this morning for a haircut and I tried to get a sports jacket but they are sold out. Did some digging at the back. Dick and Suzanne came for tea, also McNay, Mother and daughter. He brought glasses for Audrey to use tomorrow. Audrey looked smart in Gill's cast off red stripe blouse.

Tuesday, 2nd June 1953

Wet and bitterly cold. Audrey left 5.40am. The children were very good all day. Mike went in for his first race (last but one). Audrey came back at 7pm. She had a fine time – saw the Queen twice and all the rest of them including Sir Winston. We put Dave in his pram and went to the local in the evening. The kids got a mug and ball pen each.

Wednesday, 3rd June 1953

Cold and wet still. Miserable at work. Audrey's Mum came up. She and Bill spent the whole day indoors reading and listening to the wireless. I think they wish they had seen the TV. Did a bit of lashing in the garden and sowed some more lettuce. Planted our Suttons Calendula raised by Audrey's Father.

Thursday, 4th June 1953
Cold and wet. Both children vaccinated this afternoon. Both in the right arm. The lettuce Mr Baker gave me have been most useful. Our first sowing could be cut small now to thin the rows.

Friday, 5th June 1953
Rather warmer today. David has developed a cold. Mac and Dick came up this evening. Mac said Suzanne has a bad cold so we reckon David caught hers. Sticked the main crop Onward peas and weeded all the small stuff which is coming on well.

Saturday, 6th June 1953
Fine sunny day. Worked in the garden at the back all day. Went to see my Mother with Gillian this evening. She is progressing well. Afterwards Don took Audrey and me to see Windsor Castle floodlit. David's cold is quite bad. Lent my mother 'Gone Afield'.

Sunday, 7th June 1953
Dull and cloudy all day. Cut the grass at the front in ½ hour. Mike has developed the cold now. A real streamer. We have been woken several times the last two nights by one or other of them. David's vaccination is just beginning to develop on his arm.

Monday, 8th June 1953
Sunny but with a cold wind. The children are no worse but both Audrey and I have bits of colds. Mike's vaccination is beginning to act today. Did a very small bit of hoeing only this evening.

Tuesday, 9th June 1953
Fine. Did a lot of hoeing at the back this evening. Gill and Don came up with a lot of chips which we all pigged. Listened to the big fight; Turpin beat Humez.

Wednesday, 10th June 1953
Warm day. Audrey's Mother and Father came up this evening. Cut the big privet hedge at the front. Hard work – had to trim it back about 2 feet in places.

Thursday, 11th June 1953
Dull, rather wet day. Went to the Annual Dinner – rather a dull affair. Drove round London to see the lights afterwards. I have never seen so many coaches in my life. Arrived home 2am. First test match with Australia started today.

Friday, 12th June 1953
Sold 6 Budgies to Jones & Rivetts. Very tired tonight – no gardening. There has been no let up on grass cutting this year with all the damp and no opportunity so far for the children to wear bathing costumes.

Saturday, 13th June 1953
Dull and damp. Went to London this morning and bought a suit from Austin Reeds. London is very crowded. Went next door after dinner to see a fancy dress display by the children. Mike was Wee Willie Winkie in one of my old shirts. Went to see my Mother who came out of hospital today.

Sunday, 14th June 1953
Very close and damp. Did a little bit of digging this morning. Felt rather queer after dinner so went to bed and slept for 3 hours. My father came up this evening – Mother is getting on alright.

Monday, 15th June 1953
Nice morning but pouring from midday with violent thunderstorm that has put the lights out. No cricket at Nottingham. I went with Audrey's Mother and Father to see the Coronation film – very good! The children's colds are about better but Dave is cutting a double tooth.

Tuesday, 16th June 1953
   Thoroughly wet day but cleared up this evening sufficiently to do some more hedge cutting at Smiths side.

Wednesday, 17th June 1953
   Showers and bright periods. Audrey's Mother came up this afternoon. Jack Darvill and his wife called in this evening. We had our first picking of broad beans. DELICIOUS. Cherries and broad beans are about 3 weeks behind last year. It is a poor summer so far.

Thursday, 18th June 1953
   Better day at last. Audrey took Dave and Mike to be immunized. Mike says his leg hurts tonight. He is very hot and flushed and can't get to sleep.

Friday, 19th June 1953
   Dull day with showers. Mike refused to walk all day because of his leg. We are quite worried although I think he is putting it on a bit. Audrey cut the front grass. The pigeons have eaten most of my brussels.

Saturday, 20th June 1953
   Nice day. Audrey had her hair permed. Fracas with the Co-Op. Mike and Dave very good. We had to force Mike to run round the garden this morning otherwise he wouldn't have got on his feet. He has hobbled round all day. Staked the runners and made a scarecrow for the pigeons. Planted out Savoys.

Sunday, 21st June 1953
   Dull day with torrential rain at night. Mike's leg is OK now. Peg and John and my Father came up this evening.

Monday, 22nd June 1953
   Nice day. Spent the evening weeding the flower beds. The weeds are growing like mad. The Lupins are passing by. The roses are very nice now. Most of the new ones are growing well. The Giant Stride peas are coming into flower.

Tuesday, 23rd June 1953

Very sunny, warm day. Went round to Mr Baker's this evening. He gave me tomato, celery and Carnation plants. We have had the odd raspberry today.

Wednesday, 24th June 1953

Very close and hot today. Digging, weeding and planting out this evening. The Wild Honeysuckle in the hedge gives out a wonderful scent. The cherries are beginning to ripen. Audrey went into town today. Had to pay £1 for her false tooth – we are broke again! Ordered 1 ton coal and 1 ton anthracite.

Thursday, 25th June 1953

Glorious hot day. Mac and Suzanne came up for the day. Gill and Don in the evening. Don, Dick and I went for a drink. We sat in the garden of the Green Man. Trimmed the front privet hedge again. My Grandfather had to go into Wycombe Hospital for an emergency operation today.

Friday, 26th June 1953

Up at 6.30am hoeing this morning. Another hot day. Mike and Dave about in shorts and napkins only. Ordered gate posts from Kearley and fixed up with Mr Baldwin for cement and ballast. Mac and Dick are coming up Sunday to help fix the gates. Hoeing and bonfires this evening. Audrey has trained the Clematis. Dave's vaccination scab got knocked off this evening. Picked a few cherries but not really ripe yet.

Saturday, 27th June 1953

Cooler and sunny today. I went to see my Mother first thing. My Grandfather had a successful operation. Cut all of the grass this morning. Went to Peg's birthday party. Lovely tea: ham, fruit, cream and cream cakes, cheese straws etc. Planted Ridge cucumber, sowed beet and lettuce Tom Thumb.

Sunday, 28th June 1953

Torrential rain first thing. Dull morning. Very hot and sunny in the afternoon. Dick, Mac and Suzanne came for the day. We erected the concrete gate posts by 5pm. Hard work! David has been crawling in earnest today for about the first time.

Monday, 29th June 1953
Fine warm day. Took Mike to his Nan Nan's. Cutting down dead flowers, weeding and hoeing in readiness for the holiday. Dick brought Laurie up late this evening to quote for reupholstering the suite. No cheaper than Holloway.

Tuesday, 30th June 1953
Hot and close again. Awful atmosphere at Harrisons. More gardening, weeding etc. Gill and Don came for a Bean Bacon and New Potato Supper. Voted excellent all round. Marvellous last day of the Test Match; Watson and Bailey saved England.

Wednesday, 1st July 1953
Hot still. Audrey's Mother and Father brought the trunk up this evening and stayed talking about the holiday. It is just beginning to get exciting.

Thursday, 2nd July 1953
Dull and cooler today. Played hospitals with Mike and Frances. Cut the grass at the back. Can't do any more to the gates as I am waiting for Syneds to send the wood. Wrote to have the cesspool emptied.

Friday, 3rd July 1953
Dull at first but warm and sunny later. Audrey went into Wycombe to do some holiday shopping. Picked cherries in the evening. The crop isn't as good as last year and the birds have had a lot. The greens that were eaten by the birds are growing again. David will get uncovered these nights. We tuck him up about 3 times.

Saturday, 4th July 1953
Fine warm day. I went to Wycombe and brought the gateposts back by taxi!! Spent the rest of the day erecting the gates. Mac, Dick and Ben came up in the evening and we went on a pub crawl. Mac looked after the kids – Suzanne slept on our bed. The Kings Head, the Saracens Head, the Crown and the Royal Standard.

Sunday, 5th July 1953

Glorious hot day. Fiddled in the garden and worked on the gates – final touches etc. My father and Aunt Olive came up this morning. They had been to get some cherries. Audrey's Mum and Pop came up this evening and we talked holidays.

Monday, 6th July 1953

Dull and cooler with some rain. Peg and John are in Cornwall this week. Spent the evening hoeing and grass cutting. Our row of Giant Stride peas will be ready while we are on holiday. Fertilized the melon plants which are in flower. The Spiraea is full out. It is very good this year – the rain suits it.

Tuesday, 7th July 1953

Dull and cool with showers. The trunk went today. Gill and Don came up to say they won't be staying here as they are moving into a flat on Monday. Mike has a cold – bother! He chose tonight to make himself a bed of damp blankets! More hoeing and grass cutting. There is about one more picking of broad beans. Gillian's Carnation is out – very pretty.

Wednesday, 8th July 1953

Very cool with a strong wind which has broken off my rose graft. Have mended it with raffia and grafting wax and hoping for the best. Audrey's Mother came up and brought us 5½ lbs strawberry jam. We cut all of the grass at the front and did most of the packing. Mike's cold is not bad but Dave has developed it now – blast!

Thursday, 9th July 1953

Cool and showery. General clearing up in the garden. My Mother came up. The Test Match (Number 3) started today at Manchester. As usual, little play because of rain.

Friday, 10th July 1953

Fine warm day. Flogged 6 Budgies. £4.10.0d. Very busy at work but have cleared all up. Worked hard tonight packing, bathing etc. Mike woke up every hour until midnight and wanted to know if it was time to get up!

Saturday, 11th July 1953

Fine at first. Set off with Mac and Dick at 6.30am from Marlow. Good trip. Parted from Dick at Blandford. Reached Branscombe 12.20pm. 150 miles. It started to rain and has poured all the rest of the day. Giant waves. Mike and Dave both very good and their colds are a lot better. Audrey's cold is getting better. It is now 8pm and we are straight – the kids are asleep.

Wednesday 15th July 1953

I am starting to write this on Wednesday evening. The weather has been quite reasonable with plenty of sunshine but a continual strong westerly wind and showers. It has been ideal for flying Mike's kite Bill bought. We have spent most of the time on the beach near the chalets but on Tuesday morning we went into Sidmouth where we had our dinner and bought various goods. Dave's cold is practically better today and he looks very well. Mike has a bit of a throat and he has been very quiet today. Mike has been extremely good all of the time but Dave has been rather grizzly to say the least. He seems to have settled down now, thank goodness. The beer is not too good at the Masons Arms though the cider is excellent. This morning we went exploring to Castle Rock and I saw and tried to kill an adder. This afternoon we went to the rocks in the other direction. Bill and I had a dip – no more as it was very cold or seemed so to us. I made a net and caught some shrimps and prawns which we cooked this evening. They smell and look good though I don't fancy them much. We had a card from Mac and Dick today. They have a nice place and are enjoying themselves. I expect I shall stay at home this evening to read 'The Cruel Sea' while Audrey goes for a drink. Audrey it seems is going to Beer tonight for some fish and chips and is going to bring some back, I hope. Mike visits his Nan Nan 2 or 3 times a day beginning immediately after breakfast at about 8am. He is quite happy here and doesn't want to go home.

Thursday, 16th July 1953
Cold and pouring with rain all the morning. We all went into Seaton this morning shopping and got thoroughly wet. Strangely the afternoon was fine and we sat around and did nothing in particular. Mike wouldn't eat his dinner. Bill and I went for a drink to the Three Horseshoes. Very swanky. Dave very good.

Friday, 17th July 1953
Cold wind blowing off the sea but the sun has been shining all day. Audrey has had her bathing costume on but only because Mike tipped a bucket of water over her and she had to change into something. Mike wouldn't eat his dinner again. We have had a very quiet day sitting about reading.

Saturday, 18th July 1953
Wonderful hot sunny morning, lying on the beach fishing – without success of course. Violent rainstorm at midday. Went to Beer in the afternoon. I walked back along the cliffs. The evening was very pleasant and Audrey and I went to the Masons Arms while Bill and Elsie looked after the kids. It made quite a change. This certainly seems a nice long holiday.

Sunday, 19th July 1953
Fine hot day but rain this evening. I had a swim this morning. Very nice dinner of chops, green peas and marrow. Spent most of the day lazing about in the sun. I had 2 pints of delicious cider and took Audrey back a miniature rum. Audrey is looking and feeling very energetic.

Monday, 20th July 1953
Terrible dull morning with a black mist on the cliffs – we went into Sidmouth shopping. Walked out of the Radway and the Three Horseshoes on the way back – dozy service. Got a quick one at the Masons. Bill and I walked along the cliff path and found a ruined building covered with ivy and saw two adders. Lovely afternoon and evening. Went to see Childs at the Ship at Axmouth in the evening.

Tuesday, 21st July 1953
Another dull day – spent the morning climbing the cliff above Ford's House. Wild flowers galore. Sat around in the heat playing with the kids and reading. Mike sent a card to Frances. Audrey went to Beer and had some more fish and chips!! She has put on 9lbs!! I think she regrets it.

Wednesday, 22nd July 1953
Dull and showery at Branscome. We went on a trip to Dawlish, Teignmouth (worth a holiday visit), Babbacombe, Torquay and Brixham and Cockington. Had a drink at the Smugglers Inn outside Dawlish and the Drum Inn at Cockington. Stuck our name and address in a crevice in the Old Forge. Don't know why. Had a cream and fruit tea on the way home – arrived back in a terrific rainstorm although the weather had been lovely at Torquay. The gardens are sub-tropical and beautiful – everybody tired tonight (10 hours travelling) except the kids who refuse to go to sleep.

Thursday, 23rd July 1953
Nice day with only one rainstorm at dinner time. Audrey, Mike, Bill and I went snake hunting in the afternoon. Killed 2 adders and missed 3 or 4 more. Audrey and I stayed in this evening.

Friday, 24th July 1953
Fine hot day – the first and only without any rain. Audrey, Mike, Dave and I went to the Masons for cider and orange squash at lunch time. Audrey, Mike and I went in the sea in the afternoon but it was too rough to swim. Mike got a mouthful.

Saturday, 25th July 1953
Fine morning, fortunately. Packing – loading the car, getting the luggage up the cliffs etc – damned hard work. Left at 12.30pm. Met Peg and John at Stonehenge at 4pm. Traffic extremely heavy. Arrived home 7pm. Audrey thought she had lost her purse but hadn't. Everybody tired and hungry. The house was stuffy and airless but we soon settled down. Frances and Gillian were round within 5 minutes. Dave and Mike went to bed about 9pm.

Sunday, 26th July 1953

Fine morning but wet after dinner. Managed to cut the grass at the front before the rain. Fortunately things haven't grown too much. Audrey did all the washing, dried and ironed and all. Gill and Don came up in the evening. Don went out and bought us supper of egg, chips and brawn from Madge's Café!! My Mother and Father went to Weston-Super-Mare on Friday. I don't know for how long.

Monday, 27th July 1953

Showery day. Needless to say work was awful. Audrey cut some grass during the day and we planted out Wallflowers in the evening. Mike and Dave have been good. Both are eating well. Mike has been playing with Frances all day – she is on her summer holidays now.

Tuesday, 28th July 1953

Better day – rather close and warm. Audrey has cut more grass. After working in the garden this evening it seems to be coming under control. We are short of greens. The beans are setting, also marrows and there will shortly be some peas. We have some nice carrots however. Picked an Early Rivers plum.

Wednesday, 29th July 1953

Not a bad day but a wet evening. Audrey's Mother had to borrow a coat to go home in the rain. We were unable to go in the garden this evening. Blast the weather. One of the young Budgies died and one of the breeding cocks has disappeared – most mysterious. There are a lot of mice in the aviaries.

Thursday, 30th July 1953

Bright intervals. Mike and Dave immunized today. Mike was not too keen but he bought himself a pink ice cream afterwards and soon got over it. Made 13lbs of blackcurrant jam this evening.

Friday, 31st July 1953

Pouring wet day but the evening was fine. Met my Father in Wycombe – he had just returned from Weston and looked very well. Started to clear a space under the apple tree for Suttons Excelsior Hybrid Foxgloves. Apart from a slightly stiff leg, Mike is not too badly after his 'prick' yesterday. Bottled 4lbs blackcurrants.

Saturday, 1st August 1953

Fine warm day. I took Mike into Wycombe this morning. Worked in the garden weeding and grass trimming etc. Planted out Foxgloves. Audrey and I went to Gomms Wood for the first time. Very much impressed.

Sunday, 2nd August 1953

Glorious hot day. Mike playing with the kids next door – all day. Picked Early Rivers plums for tart, also a small picking of runners for Mike's dinner. Pulled buckets of weeds up. Wearing shorts and singlet – even Audrey wore shorts this morning. Father brought us some Turkish Delight this evening.

Monday, 3rd August 1953 (Bank Holiday)

Fine warm day. Shorts and bathing costumes! No visitors. As a consequence we have done a lot of gardening – cut all the grass and the back hedge. Trimmed the front privet hedge, hoed and weeded. As a consequence the garden is now in excellent shape. David has been very good and Michael spent most of the day next door – he even had his tea there.

Tuesday, 4th August 1953

Warm and dry. The case arrived today and we spent the whole evening washing – every line filled and still there are nine sheets to hang out!! Audrey put on 8lbs during the holiday and has started to diet today. No bread or potatoes or sweets or pastry!

Wednesday, 5th August 1953

Fine and very close. Audrey's Mother came up as usual and Bill fetched her. Sowed Spring Cabbage Wheelers Imperial and planted out a few Violas. I had beans and marrow for my dinner tonight. Audrey is feeling hungry – hard luck!
Waist 28¾", tummy 37", hips 38¾", bust 36¾".

Thursday, 6th August 1953

Dry dull and close day. Audrey is still dieting and complains of hunger. Fortunately, she is able to raid the plum trees. Tried to light the bonfire without success. Played a game of darts which Audrey won and did some hoeing. Sowed Arctic King lettuce (I am afraid this will be too late for autumn use, sowed 7th July last – still I shall use cloches and it might do the trick).

Friday, 7th August 1953

Fine hot day. Gill and Don went on their holiday yesterday. We seem to have a melon set. I am wearing just shorts and vest these evenings. Getting quite brown on top of the holiday. Peg and John came this evening. We played a game of darts outside. Peg is having a baby in February.

Saturday, 8th August 1953

Fine hot day. Audrey had her hair set this morning and afterwards I went into work. Mac and Dick came up in the afternoon and stayed overnight. Spent most of the afternoon practising golf on the lawn in the course of which I knocked out next door's cat!

Sunday, 9th August 1953

Very hot day. No shirts all day. Mac and Dick left early. Boiled beef and carrots for dinner. Mike and Frances in bathing costumes playing with the hose pipe this afternoon. Very little gardening done this weekend. This weather is the best of the summer so far.

Monday, 10th August 1953

Another hot day. Gill and Don are having good weather. Had a card from Polperro today. Hoeing, grass cutting and watering in the garden this evening. David took his first steps today. He is into everything. Every knob or bit of wire is fair game! Mike plays with Frances all day, every day.

Tuesday, 11th August 1953

Fine and warm. This hot weather is ideal for the plums although generally I believe the crop is poor – they are 8d lb in the shops.

Wednesday, 12th August 1953

Hottest day since 1948. Shocking at work. Audrey's Mother came up today and Bill came up in the evening. We went for a drink in the garden of the Green Man. Audrey's Mother had 7lbs and my Mother 6lbs plums. Cordyline Australis is the palm like plant one sees at Bournemouth.

Thursday, 13th August 1953

Not quite so hot today, thank goodness. I bought a new shower-proof coat. We bottled about 5lbs plums. The plums need picking every evening to prevent the insects and birds eating them. My Mother had a few more plums this evening and took some runners for her dinner tomorrow.

Friday, 14th August 1953

Hot and dry still. Audrey and the children went into Wycombe today. She bought some curtains for Mike's room but doesn't like them now she has got them! David still does the occasional step. Audrey has got her weight down to 9s 11½ lbs. Weeding and watering tonight. Several tomatoes are nearly ripe.

Saturday, 15th August 1953
Wet morning. Generally dull day. Test Match weather again. I went into Wycombe and bought a hat and shoes. Spent the afternoon making Mike's curtains. My Mother came up this evening while Audrey and I went out. We had a drink in Wycombe and looked in the shops. Afterwards we looked in at Flackwell Fair. Got back home and cooked bacon and eggs. Took 2 Budgies to Tilley.

Sunday, 16th August 1953
Fine sunny day but with a distinct nip in the air this morning. Spent nearly all day clearing a stoppage in the rainwater pipe by the bathroom. In the end I broke the pipe and black water spurted all over Mike. Gill and Don came up this evening. They look well after their holiday. They brought me a large pipe and Audrey a necklace and rock for the kids.

Monday, 17th August 1953
Fine and sunny. We have today bought an Aladdin oil radiator. £10. I took my overcoat back to have the sleeves shortened slightly. We spent the evening making jam and pickling onions. We have decided now that sugar is supposed to be coming off the ration to make all our jam.

Tuesday, 18th August 1953
Fine sunny day although it rained in the night. Started to prepare the patch, where Mayhew's garage was, for grass. Audrey's Mother came up to say that she wouldn't be up tomorrow as Peggy was unwell. Cesspool emptied today.

Wednesday, 19th August 1953
Dull day with showers. Audrey's mother didn't come up today as she went to Peggy who is expecting the doctor. I collected 2 yellow Budgies on an exchange basis from 'The Chalet' this evening and Audrey went to see Peggy who is OK! To date, we have made or had given to us the following quantities of jams: 4lbs raspberry, 5lbs strawberry, 1lb apricot, 13lbs blackcurrant, 11lbs plum.

Thursday, 20th August 1953

Dull day with showers. Violent rain last night. Syneds collected the hinges and Stevens delivered 28lbs bird seed which we started using from now. Audrey's Mother and Pop came up this evening. They had some plums and a marrow. No gardening the last 2 evenings as it has been dull and rather discouraging. Dark by 9pm tonight. Lords delivered Aladdin – seems to be good.

Friday, 21st August 1953

Rather dull and showery. I collected a hen (green) Budgie with 5 eggs from Coppuck tonight. It was a wet evening with thunder; consequently we were unable to do any gardening. The garden is getting rather untidy with all this wet we have had and the odd jobs, jam making etc. The front hedge needs cutting. I must do it this autumn. The Fuschia has been poor this year.

Saturday, 22nd August 1953

Dull cool day. I went into Wycombe twice this morning: once to collect my Mac from the cleaners and to take in several other things, and the second time to take 2 Budgies into Tilley. In the afternoon mended a hole in the roof over Mike's bedroom and painted everything in sight with aluminium paint. Of course, Mike touched it to see if it was dry. My Mother came up this evening. She brought Mike and David a ball each – we have lots and lots now. She had some plums. They are 1/- lb now. Tilley is paying 15/- for Budgies.

Sunday, 23rd August 1953

Miserable thoroughly wet day. Nobody has been out all day. The beans are extremely prolific (we salted down about 3lbs today). Bottled some more plums including the first of the Victorias. Next door's cat has spent the day with us. The children have been very good and Mike and I have been wrestling.

Monday, 24th August 1953

Showery weather. Our beans have gone all watery so we have chucked them.

Tuesday, 25th August 1953
Fine day. Planted out quite a large strawberry bed with plants given us by Audrey's Mother.

Wednesday, 26th August 1953
Fine day. Audrey's Mother and Father came up this evening.

Thursday, 27th August 1953
Fine day. Michael went to the doctors and had a jolly good yell and kick. His leg is stiffening up. David quite unaffected. We made 7lbs Victoria jam.

Friday, 28th August 1953
Fine day. Audrey went into Wycombe this morning – Mike is hobbling everywhere and his leg is quite swollen. I took some plums to my Mother this evening (my Father tells me that my Aunt Gertie has gone into hospital for some operation).

Saturday, 29th August 1953
Pouring with rain continuously all day. I went into Wycombe to do some shopping in the morning. Spent the afternoon painting and Rentokiling Mike's room. Spent the evening reading and listening to the wireless. Mike's leg has been a lot better today although he limps a bit.

Sunday, 30th August 1953
Fine and sunny. Finished off the painting and continued clearing the ground by the big Laurel ready for grassing. My Father came up in the evening and Mike staged a terrific scene shouting and screaming because I took the gramophone records from him. Made 12lbs Victoria jam.

Monday, 31st August 1953
Fine day. Audrey cut all of the grass at the front. Bought a dozen eggs and 6lbs of greengages off Smith. Made 6lbs greengage jam this evening. Had one reply to my book advert today. Tomlin – coach building at Amersham.

Tuesday, 1st September 1953
>Lovely warm day and evening. Frances has gone back to school today and Mike has been playing quite happily by himself in the garden. Gillian came up for a few minutes this evening and took some Foxglove plants for her woodland garden. Spent the evening clearing and hedge cutting by the Laurel – it is a big job but will be a great improvement to the garden. Took Audrey's Mother about 10lbs Victorias.

Wednesday, 2nd September 1953
>Cool and showery. Audrey's Mother came up as usual and Bill fetched her. We bottled 2 jars of greengages and one of damsons. Write to Waterer's regarding Veronica Speciosa evergreen hybrid with red or purple flowers.

Thursday, 3rd September 1953
>Nice sunny day. Audrey took Mike and Dave into Fennels Wood this afternoon. The 2 jars of gages did not take. They were not sufficiently filled with fruit, I think. Posted book to Mr Tomlin today. Still working on the grass patch by the Laurel.

Friday, 4th September 1953
>Wet morning but nice later. Audrey and the children went to Wycombe. She bought a nightdress for Peg's baby. We had a good bonfire tonight. The rubbish has been difficult to get rid of this year owing to the wet. Gillian and Don came up and returned the tent. Groundsheet and bucket to come.

Saturday, 5th September 1953
>Fine sunny day. Mike got his dressing table today from Audrey's Mother. I went into Wycombe this morning – bought Audrey some nylons. Went blackberrying with Audrey's Mum and Dad to Turville. Picked 3¾ lbs and made 11lbs jam. Mac, Dick and Ben came up this evening. Ben is going to do the hall. I went out with Dick and Ben and Mr & Mrs Evans to the Black Lion and Green Man. Came back afterwards and sat about until midnight.

Sunday, 6th September 1953

Fine hot day. General clearing up, weeding and bonfire making in the garden all day. No visitors, thank goodness. David has been off colour and rather grizzly. We have made 70lbs of jam to date. We are hoping for an Indian Summer after today's weather.

Monday, 7th September 1953

Glorious hot day. Finished preparing the patch to be grassed by the Laurel. We had very bad luck on our first attempt at 3 draws on Saturday.

Tuesday, 8th September 1953

Glorious hot day. Instead of working I took a Budgie to Mr Saunders at Loudwater and got lost in Fennels Wood! Sent to Ryders for 4½ lbs grass seed for 10/-. This has been one of the best spells of the summer.

Wednesday, 9th September 1953

Cooler but fine. Worked in the garden until it was dark at 8pm. Cut all the grass and reshaped the grass by the path. Audrey's Mother and Father came up and stayed awhile. Had another reply about my books from Mr Laird. He is interested in the lot. Audrey planted out Linum and Verbascum seedlings.

Thursday, 10th September 1953

Fine and cool and very cold tonight. My Mother came up this evening. Aunt Gertie is in convalescent home at Nettlebed and Uncle John is in hospital at Harefield. Peg and John came up later and stayed quite late. Mike and Dave played switching the wireless on and off. First time I have seen Dave consciously playing a game. He kept saying 'again' and grinned all over his face.

Friday, 11th September 1953

Fine sunny day. Audrey and the children went into Wycombe again today. We sowed the grass by the Laurel at the front. Gillian and Don came up this evening. Don brought his exam questions to show us.

Saturday, 12th September 1953
Fine day but dull. I went into Wycombe again and got my saw. It cut so well that we had an orgy of tree felling. The old apple tree by Mike's room and part of the large Sycamore in Mr Smith's garden. We had a tremendous bonfire with the foliage and have lots of wood for fires. The garden looks quite different.

Sunday, 13th September 1953
Fine sunny day. Started to clear under the Cox's for grass. Sat in the garden this afternoon – hope not the last time this year. This month has been very dry and sunny so far. The Fuschia is flowering its best now. I think we have more vegetables this year than before. Cut a cauliflower today, also 2 cucumbers.

Monday, 14th September 1953
Fine warm sunny day. Spent the evening sowing grass under the Silver Birch at the front and touching up various bad patches. I'm afraid it will take a few years before the lawn is much like one. Mike has made the garden look like a scrap dealer's yard today.

Tuesday, 15th September 1953
Fine day with rain this evening after dark. Cut the hedge at the back and planted Wallflowers round the house. I wrote to Mr Davies today about the BIM (British Institute of Management). We have 3 young birds which have been pecked bare of feathers around the neck.

Wednesday, 16th September 1953
Rather dull with showers and fine this evening. David's first birthday. 12 cards including a greetings telegram. Many presents, mostly clothes. All very nice indeed. Also a teddy bear and a panda. Mike has been very good and not a bit jealous. He had a card from Mrs Foster and Audrey's Father bought him an Alice in Wonderland rug.

Thursday, 17th September 1953
David completely abandoned crawling yesterday – his birthday. He walks all the time now. He still has only 6 teeth. Mike sounds his aitches at last. He is still hard to understand because he will gabble so. He is able to fill the bath – get in and he can wash his hair after a fashion.

Friday, 18th September 1953
> Rather dull. Planted out Sweet Williams (not very good plants this year) and Wallflowers. Audrey spent the evening making trifles and icing cakes.

Saturday, 19th September 1953
> Rather dull showery day. Spent the morning humping furniture around in readiness for the party. The tea was good and everyone seemed to enjoy themselves including David and Mike. We played the usual games including Mother McGie. My Father was unable to come. He had been to see both my Auntie and Uncle in hospital.

Sunday, 20th September 1953
> Fine sunny day. Planted out Spring Cabbage and Arctic King lettuce plants. Stole some cuttings of Russian Vine. We all went for a walk this afternoon – saw some council house being put up at Heath End. Gill took 2 Budgies. Mike, Frances and Gill played at fishing in the shrub border.

Monday, 21st September 1953
> Fine sunny day. Took Mike to his Nan Nan's. When he got home tonight he had a funny tummy and demanded something to make it better. Gave him some Macleans which he drank.

Tuesday, 22nd September 1953
> Mike has developed a cold today, worse luck. I expect we shall all catch it, as usual. Goodness knows where he got it from. He now makes an attempt to draw a house by doing a rough square with some scribble for windows etc.

Wednesday, 23rd September 1953
> Fine day. Audrey's Mother came up as usual but Bill was working. Had an offer from Coulton today. David has learned to wave 'ta ta' and I must say he is most responsive. The grass we sowed on the 14th of this month is well up.

Thursday, 24th September 1953
Mac and Dick and Suzanne came up today. Mac and Suzanne stayed the day. They gave David some money for his money box. Ben may be coming down in a fortnight's time. Dick hopes he may have some tiles.

Friday, 25th September 1953
Fine day. I was lucky enough to get a piece of Formica to make a table top for the kitchen. Have done very little in the garden these last few evenings. By the time the children are in bed it is dark.

Saturday, 26th September 1953
Fine hot sunny day. I went into Wycombe this morning to take Audrey's costume to be cleaned. Planted out some Michelmas Daisies given us by Mrs Agar. Went with Gill and Don and Mike to Hutchins Barn to the pre-sale viewing. A wonderful house and gardens. Managed to scrounge one or two seedlings and cuttings. Spent most of the evening working on the kitchen table. My Mother looked after Dave this afternoon. She managed very well.

Sunday, 27th September 1953
Fine day. Started digging round the blackcurrant bushes. Planted out Lychnis Chal and moved several herbaceous plants. We have all got colds today and rather choppered as a result. We have beans, marrow, cucumber, brussels, cabbage, cauliflower, carrots, onions, Swedes, kohl rabi, lettuce, celery, tomatoes, parsnips all ready!!!

Monday, 28th September 1953
Fine sunny day but the mornings and evenings are chilly. I cut the grass this evening and wrote to Drayson. David's cold is much better. Audrey spent the evening making cakes and tarts because Bridget is coming to tea tomorrow.

Friday, 2nd October 1953
Fine day. Audrey and the children went into Wycombe. Audrey bought some shoes from the Co-Op.

Saturday, 3rd October 1953

Fine hot day. Nobody went out and I spent the whole day clipping the front hedge and grass verge. The garden looks very nice now. The Fuschia continues to flower profusely. Nothing has been touched by frost and very few leaves have fallen from the trees.

Sunday, 4th October 1953

Fine and sunny but cooler. Spent the morning weeding and grass clipping at the front.

Monday, 5th October 1953

Cold and fine. It was nice and easy to get up this morning now the clocks are back. Wrote to Stuart McClean, or rather posted the letter today. Audrey cut the grass at the back. I don't think it will need doing again. Won the football pool at work. 35/-.

Tuesday, 6th October 1953

Cold and fine. We had our first fire today – in the drawing room. There was a frost today in places. We didn't have one here though. Sent a reminder to Laird about the books.

Wednesday, 7th October 1953

Audrey's mother came up as usual and Bill collected her in the evening. Bill rediscovered one of his boyhood poems 'I remember, I remember'.

Friday, 9th October 1953

Fine day. Audrey and the children went into Wycombe. I had a letter from Stuart McClean offering to see me.

Saturday, 10th October 1953

Fine day. Worked in the back garden all day. Digging and clearing up in general. Work is well forward for the time of year. Dick and Ben came up this evening. Went for a drink. I am worried about getting time off next week.

Sunday 11th October 1953
Fine hot day. Rough digging by the blackcurrants. Went for a walk this afternoon just around the square. Mike delighted in pretending David is a monkey and caging him in with chair and cushions. David is difficult to hold.

Tuesday, 13th October 1953
Wet day, the first this month. Gill and Don came up this evening. They brought us a good specimen Rhododendron and also their shelves they bought at the sale for us to see. White elephant alright!

Wednesday, 14th October 1953
Dull and rather damp. Saw McClean this morning. Quite an experience. I fancy that I haven't much hope. Saw Drayson afterwards. He is going to speak to Paul on my behalf. Lunch with Hodder and back to the grind this afternoon.

Thursday, 15th October 1953
Fine day but rather cold and damp. We have lit the fire in the kitchen. This is official start of winter. Out to lunch with Don today. He was keen to know how I got on yesterday.

Friday, 16th October 1953
Fine sunny day. Not so cold. This is certainly an excellent October so far.

Saturday, 17th October 1953
Dull day with drizzle. I went with my Mother to the unveiling of the Runneymede Memorial on Coopers Hill. It was unfortunate that the weather was so poor. Went out with Audrey this evening. First time for ages. Had a few Worthingtons in the Dragon and thoroughly enjoyed it.

Sunday, 18th October 1953

Fine day. Spent nearly all day in the garden. Digging and clearing up etc. No visitors. We haven't had a frost yet. There is still an occasional picking of beans.

Monday, 19th October 1953

Fine but dull. Of all things, Tryngham offered me an introduction to LTA. Audrey has had a bad day. Sink blocked up and the chair cushion caught on fire.

Monthly Income

£ 5. 0. 0   Cash (Budgie Sales)
£ 3. 0. 0   Family Allowance
£ 2. 0. 0   Co-op Dividend
£ 47. 10. 0   Wage cheque
_____

£ 57. 10 .0

Monthly Expenses

£ 17. 10. 0   Electric light and cooker (cooker on HP)
£ 10. 17. 6   House
£ 7. 0. 0   Bank
£ 14. 0. 0   Jennings (local shop, monthly account)
£   15. 0   Jones & Rivetts (Budgie supplies)
£ 2. 10. 0   Insurance
£ 3. 0. 0   Coal
£ 10. 0. 0   Housekeeping
£ 1. 5. 0   Miscellaneous
_____
£ 66. 17. 6
£   10. 0   Mr Coppuck (Budgie supplies)
_____
£ 67. 7. 6

£ 57. 10. 0   Less Income
_____

£ 10. 0. 0   Deficit plus water rates